OFF THE

BONE

OFF THE
BONE

NEW HOLLAND

Contents

Introduction

Off The Bone

Ah, meat. For a carnivore, there is nothing more satisfying than a pink and succulent T-bone steak, the sizzle of well-seasoned chicken on a barbecue, or a serve of crispy, roast pork crackling.

Off The Bone gives both classic and contemporary recipes for cooking 'bone-in meat'—that is, meat that hasn't been filleted, and is cooked and served with the bone included. From warming childhood favourites like lamb shanks and osso bucco to spicy chicken wings and smoky pork ribs, this is the recipe book for anyone who loves meat and wants to try cooking it in new and interesting ways.

The benefits of these cuts are endless. The bone acts as a heat-conductor, so the meat cooks more evenly, but still retains its juiciness. The cuts are typically cheaper, but no less tasty than their filleted counterparts, so offer great value. Spices, garlic, butter and other seasonings can be stuffed under chicken skin, or between the meat and the bone, for an extra flavour kick. And when bones are boiled, they release gelatin, which makes stews and soups incredibly tasty.

Recipes in this book are suitable for both novice and experienced cooks. If you're ever at a loss for what meat to choose, your local butcher will be knowledgeable about every type and portion of meat, and can advise on what will suit your taste and needs. Don't be shy—butchers are usually friendly folk, and love to champion their favourite 'unsung' cuts! Buy local, organic and free-range to ensure the very best quality.

Whether it's a rack of lamb for a special occasion, a hearty mid-week steak, or tender veal cutlets for a family barbecue, *Off The Bone* features every recipe you might need for delicious bone-in meat.

Beef

Beef

PAN-FRYING BEEF

Points for success

* Trim steaks and chops of excess fat. Make one or two small cuts around selvedge—past the gristle line into the meat. This prevents meat curling up.

* Season with pepper and dried herbs before cooking, add salt after cooking.

* Use a small amount of oil in the pan—too much oil makes meat stew.

* A non-stick pan helps reduce the quantity of cooking fat needed, therefore reducing the fat content of the meal. Alternatively, use non-stick cooking paper to reduce the fat content and prevent the beef sticking.

* Oils or fats suitable for pan-frying are: vegetable oils, butter, ghee (clarified butter) and margarine. Butter gives a good flavour but can burn easily—it is better to use a combination of butter and oil to prevent this and still retain flavour. Ghee will not burn easily and has a distinctive and pleasant flavour.

* Heat oil and pan well. Sear meat on both sides to seal in juices, then turn down to medium-high or medium to continue cooking. Cooking time will depend on the thickness of the meat. If the cut is thick, lower the heat to allow the centre to cook. If the cut is thin, cook quickly for a short time. Stay close to the pan and adjust heat when necessary.

* Cooking times vary with the thickness of the meat and the type of pan used, but a good guide is: rare: 2–3 minutes on each side, medium: 4–6 minutes on each side, well done: 6–9 minutes on each side. Turn meat three times at the most, once only for rare.

* To test if cooked, do not cut with a knife as juices escape. Test meat by pressing with blunt tongs—the meat will be: rare: springy to touch, medium: firmer to touch, well done: very firm to touch.

* Don't turn meat too often or use too low a heat as it will stew and toughen due to lack of time and heat needed to seal in the juices. You will know if this happens, as the meat will shed its juices.

* Don't pan-fry with a lid on. The lid traps in steam, making the meat stew.

* For extra tenderness and flavour, marinate meat in a wine- or citrus-based marinade. For best results, place meat and marinade in a non-metallic dish, cover with lid and refrigerate for 2 hours or more, overnight if possible.

* Always deglaze the pan (dissolve the meat juices that have stuck to the base of the pan) with stock, water, wine, lemon or fruit juices. This makes a quick and easy sauce. Cream, sour cream or yoghurt can then be added to make a richer sauce.

* Always remember to have vegetable and rice or pasta accompaniments cooked and ready before commencing to pan-fry the meat. On completion of cooking, pan-fried meat should be served immediately.

OVEN-ROASTING BEEF

Points for success

* Trim some fat from the meat. Some fat cover is necessary to keep the meat moist during cooking.
* Remove silver skin from beef fillet to prevent curling while cooking. Tie to keep shape.
* Place meat on a rack in a roasting pan. Add a cup of water or wine to cover base of pan. This will prevent the meat juices from charring. Juices may then be used in making gravy. When liquid dries out, add a little more.
* Roasts may be placed in a roasting pan without a rack. However, ensure there is a little water in the dish. As the roast cooks, fat will melt into the dish. Insert a meat thermometer into the thickest part of the meat. This will register the internal temperature of the meat, which will indicate how cooked it is. Calculate cooking time by the weight of the meat (see chart on page 11).
* Cook small or narrow roasts at 400°F (200°C), larger roasts at 350°F (180°C).
* Oven bags keep food moist and succulent, eliminate the need to clean the oven, and reduce the amount of washing up. When using an oven bag, the cooking times per 17½oz (500g) are: rare: 20 minutes, medium: 25 minutes, well done: 30 minutes.
* Very large cuts will need turning halfway through cooking.
* Remove cooked meat from oven, cover with foil and allow to stand 15 minutes. This allows juices to settle and makes carving easier.
* Carve meat across the grain to ensure tenderness.
* To make gravy, skim fat from pan. Scrape all cooked-on juices from sides and base of pan, washing down with stock or water (the term for this is deglazing).

DEGREE OF COOKING	TIME PER 17½OZ/ 500G	INTERNAL TEMPERATURE
rare	20–25 minutes	140°F/60°C
medium	25–30 minutes	160°F/70°C
well done	30–35 minutes	170°F/75°C

Barbecuing beef

Points for success

* Lightly oil grill or plate to prevent meat sticking.
* Marinate steaks, if desired, to add flavour.
* To ensure tenderness for blade and topside steak, marinate in an acid-based marinade containing wine or citrus juices for 2 hours or more.
* When cooking, begin on high heat to seal in juices, then reduce heat, move meat to cooler part of plate or raise the grill higher off the coals.
* Cooking times are the same as for grilling.

Grilling beef

Points for success

* Choose steak that is a deep red colour, as this indicates meat has been well aged and is tender.
* Trim meat of any fat. Slash the fat line at intervals to prevent the meat curling while cooking.
* Season steaks with pepper and herbs before cooking, sprinkle with salt after cooking. For extra flavour, the steak may be rubbed with a little crushed garlic.
* To keep steak moist, brush with a little olive oil just before grilling.
* Heat grill to very hot for approximately 5 minutes before placing the meat under. Do not leave the grill pan under the heat while heating the grill. The pan should be cold when the meat is placed on it so it will not stick.
* Cooking time varies according to thickness and desired degree of cooking (see chart on page 11).
* Do not turn meat too often—it will not have time to seal in juices and will stew.
* Leave grill door open while grilling.
* Grilled meat is quick to cook and must be served immediately. Have all accompaniments prepared before meat is placed under the grill.

Pot-roasting beef

Points for success

* Select a deep, covered saucepan large enough to fit your cut of meat. For oven pot-roasting, a deep casserole with lid or a cast-iron Dutch oven are needed. The latter is the more suitable as heavy metal conducts heat better.
* Trim the fat from the meat. Tie the roast with string to retain its shape during cooking. Chuck, round and topside pot roasts are usually triangular in shape. These can still be tied to retain shape. Weigh

meat to calculate cooking time. It is not wise to pot-roast a piece of meat much larger than 3lb 5oz (1.5kg) as the heat will not penetrate enough to the centre. Pot roasts need to be well cooked to be tender, rare meat is only suitable for tender prime cuts.

* Cut larger roast into two smaller pieces.
* To seal juices, brown meat on all sides in a little hot oil, on high heat. You may prefer to do this in a shallow frying pan then transfer to the pot.
* Add enough liquid to come quarter-way up side of meat. Liquid can be stock, water, or a mixture of stock and wine.
* If vegetables such as celery, carrots or onions are added, cut into small dice so that they will disintegrate in the stock, thickening it during cooking.
* Timing is important as overcooking will toughen the meat. After the stock is added allow 40 minutes per 17½oz (500g). To test when cooked, pierce meat with a skewer—should slide in easily.
* Meat may be marinated in red wine for several hours before cooking. Use the wine later in the stock. Turn meat in marinade occasionally.
* Always cook the pot roast at a slow simmer. Never let it come to the boil as the meat may toughen.
* If there is too much liquid left in the pan when meat is cooked, remove meat and keep warm, then turn up the heat to reduce the liquid. This will also intensify the flavour of the sauce.
* Many pot roast recipes do not need thickening as the gravy thickens with its own meat juices. If thickening is added it is usually in the form of beurre manié (plain (all-purpose) flour and butter creamed together), which is stirred in small amounts into the simmering gravy. Blended cornstarch (cornflour) may also be used. Bring to the boil for 1 minute to cook the starch.
* It is best to carve thin slices of meat from the pot roast. This is very easy to do using an electric knife.

Stir-frying beef

Points for success

* If preparing your own, partly freeze the meat first—this makes it easier to cut. Trim fat from the meat then slice thinly across the grain—this ensures tenderness. Cut strips 2–3in (5–8cm) in length.
* Marinate the strips for at least 30 minutes in a mixture of cornflour (cornstarch) blended with water, soy sauce, rice wine, or dry sherry. This helps keep in juices and adds flavour.
* Stir-fry meat in small batches (7–10½oz/200–300g) to prevent meat shedding its juices.
* Have all meat and vegetables prepared and all flavourings and sauces measured before starting.
* When ready to stir-fry, add a small quantity of oil to wok or frying pan and swirl to coat base and sides.
* Heat until smoking. If a wok is not available, a heavy-based frying pan may be used. Place over the small gas ring or element so that the heat is concentrated in the centre of the pan.

Japanese Beef with Horseradish

SERVES 4

Place the steaks in a non-metallic dish. Pour over the teriyaki or soy sauce and olive oil and turn the steaks to coat. Cover and marinate for 1–2 hours in the refrigerator. Mix the crème fraîche and horseradish in a small bowl, then cover and refrigerate.

Heat a ridged cast-iron grill pan over a medium-high heat. Wipe with the peanut oil, using a folded piece of absorbent paper. Alternatively, heat the oil in a heavy-based frying pan. Add 2 steaks, reserving the marinade, then cook for 3 minutes on each side or until cooked to your liking. Remove and keep warm. Cook the remaining 2 steaks, then remove and keep warm.

Put the sliced scallions, garlic, chilli and reserved marinade into a small saucepan and heat through. Spoon over the steaks and top with a dollop of the horseradish cream and shredded scallions.

4 rump steaks, about 6oz (175g) each
4 tablespoons teriyaki or soy sauce
4 tablespoons olive oil
6 tablespoons crème fraîche
4 teaspoons horseradish cream
2 teaspoons peanut oil
7 scallions (spring onions), finely sliced, plus 1 scallion (spring onion), shredded
2 cloves garlic, chopped
¼ teaspoon chilli flakes

Steaks with Garlic Butter

*4 sirloin steaks, about 6oz (170g)
    each*
*salt and freshly ground black
    pepper*
1 tablespoon vegetable oil
GARLIC BUTTER
*3½oz (100g) butter, at room
    temperature*
*2 cloves garlic, peeled and
    crushed*
*½ cup fresh parsley, finely
    chopped*

To make the garlic butter, mix together the butter, garlic and parsley in a small bowl. Place the mixture in the middle of a piece of baking paper or cling wrap, then roll the paper or cling wrap around the butter to form a sausage shape, about 1¼in (3cm) in diameter. Twist the ends to seal, then place in the refrigerator for 1 hour to harden.

Season the steaks with salt and black pepper. Heat the oil in a large heavy-based frying pan over a medium-high heat until it starts to smoke.

Put the steaks in the pan. For a medium cooked steak, cook for 2 minutes, then turn over and cook for a further 3 minutes. For a well-done steak, cook for 3 minutes, then turn over and cook for a further 4 minutes. Cooking times vary depending on the thickness of the steaks, so insert the point of a sharp knife into the middle of one of the steaks to check that it is cooked to your liking.

Remove the butter from the refrigerator, unwrap it and discard the baking paper or cling wrap. Cut into slices and serve on top of the steaks.

Perfect T-bone Steak

Combine the garlic butter ingredients. Spoon into a small pot and set aside. Bring the steaks to room temperature. Mix the garlic, oil and salt and pepper together. Rub onto both sides of the steak. Stand for 10–15 minutes at room temperature.

Heat the barbecue until hot and oil the grill bars. Arrange the steaks and sear for 1 minute on each side. Move the steaks to the cooler part of the barbecue to continue cooking over moderate heat, or turn the heat down. If the heat cannot be reduced then elevate the steaks on a wire cake rack placed on the grill bars. Cook for a total time of 5–6 minutes for rare, 7–10 minutes for medium and 10–14 minutes for well done. Turn during cooking.

Serve on a heated steak plate and top with a dollop of garlic butter. Serve with potatoes.

NOTE
To tenderise tough meat, rub in a mixture of malt vinegar and cooking oil and allow to stand for about 2 hours.

4 T-bone steaks
2 teaspoons crushed garlic
2 teaspoons oil
salt and pepper
GARLIC BUTTER
2oz (55g) butter
1 teaspoon crushed garlic
1 tablespoon parsley flakes
2 teaspoons lemon juice

Beef Roast with Cajun Potato Cakes

SERVES 8

2 lb 12 oz (1⅓kg) standing rib
  roast of beef
salt and pepper
2 teaspoons crushed garlic
2 tablespoons flour
10oz (285g) jar tomato salsa
CAJUN POTATO CAKES
4 medium-sized potatoes, boiled
  in their jackets
55g (2oz) eggs, lightly beaten
2 teaspoons Cajun seasoning
2 tablespoons olive oil
2 tablespoons flour
½ teaspoon salt

Rub the roast with salt, pepper and crushed garlic and stand at room temperature for 20 minutes. Just before placing on the barbecue, dust all over with flour. This helps to seal in the juices. Place the salsa in a small saucepan ready for heating and prepare the potato cake mixture.

For kettle and gas hooded barbecues, cook as follows: Prepare the barbecue for indirect cooking on medium-high heat. Stand the roast on oiled grill bars over a drip tray. Cover with the lid or hood and cook for 1–1½ hours or until meat a thermometer reaches 150–160°F (65°C–70°C). Remove from the barbecue, cover with foil and stand for 20 minutes before carving.

For an electric barbecue grill: Preheat to medium-high. Stand the roast in a foil baking dish. Place a wire cake rack to stand 1in (2½cm) above the grill bars and set the roast. Cover with the hood and cook as above.

To make the Cajun potato cakes, skin the boiled potatoes and mash well. Add the eggs, Cajun seasoning, olive oil, flour and salt. Mix well and form into 16 patties using floured hands. Cook on an oiled hotplate or grill bars over direct heat for about 5 minutes on each side. Heat the salsa while the patties are cooking. Carve the roast and serve with the Cajun potato cakes and salsa.

Braised Beef in Soy

SERVES 4

Grind coriander seeds in a mortar and pestle. Mix with 4 tablespoons of water.

Purée shallots and garlic in a food processor. Heat oil in a large saucepan and sauté shallot purée with cinnamon sticks until golden.

Add coriander mixture, mashed soybean paste, sugar and cloves and sauté for two minutes. Increase heat and add beef, cooking until brown on the outside.

Add soy sauce and 8 cups water and bring to the boil, stirring occasionally. Reduce heat and simmer, partially covered, until meat is tender, approximately 2½ hours.

When tender, remove beef from liquid and set aside. Continue simmering liquid until reduced to a sauce consistency. Return beef to sauce and add bamboo shoots.

Discard cinnamon sticks and adjust seasoning with salt and pepper. Garnish with red chilli pieces and watercress and serve with steamed rice.

6 tablespoons coriander seeds
12 French shallots, finely diced
12 cloves garlic, chopped
1 tablespoon olive oil
2 cinnamon sticks
½ cup soybean paste, mashed
4 tablespoons sugar
1 teaspoon ground cloves
8 small beef shins
3 tablespoons dark soy sauce
9oz (250g) canned bamboo
  shoots, drained
salt and freshly ground black
  pepper
1 large red chilli, cut into slivers
1 cup watercress

T-bone Steak with Piri Piri Butter

2½oz (80g) butter, softened

3 cloves garlic, crushed

1 teaspoon Piri Piri seasoning

1 teaspoon parsley flakes

4 T-bone steaks, about 10½oz
   (300g) each

olive oil

salt and freshly ground black
   pepper

Combine the butter, garlic, Piri Piri seasoning and parsley in a bowl. Mix together until smooth.

Place the mixture onto plastic wrap and roll into a tube shape. Place in the refrigerator or freezer until firm.

Brush the steaks with olive oil and season with salt and pepper. Cook the steaks on the barbecue grill for 3 minutes each side or until cooked to your liking. Serve the steaks with a slice of butter, crispy potatoes and green salad.

Barbecued Beef Ribs

Cut ribs into serving pieces. Place in deep bowl. Combine soy sauce, oil, mustard, lemon juice, chilli powder, garlic and pepper. Pour marinade over ribs, and wedge a few slices of thick onions between pieces of beef. Marinate for 24 hours, turning from time to time.

Barbecue over hot coals for about 20 minutes or until done. Serve with barbecue sauce.

1½kg beef ribs
MARINADE
2 tablespoons soy sauce
6 tablespoons olive oil
2 tablespoons hot mustard
1 tablespoon lemon juice
½ teaspoon chilli powder
1 clove garlic, crushed
black pepper
1 onion, thickly sliced

Korean Barbecued Beef Ribs

12 beef ribs, 2¾in (7cm) long
MARINADE
1½ cups soy sauce
3 tablespoons sesame seeds,
    toasted
3 teaspoons sugar
1 teaspoon chilli
3 large cloves garlic, crushed

Place ribs in large plastic bag. Combine soy sauce, sesame seeds, sugar, chilli and garlic and pour over ribs.

Press air out of bag and tie top securely. Refrigerate for 4 hours, turning bag over occasionally.

Remove ribs and barbecue 4in (10cm) from hot coals for about 15 minutes, or until ribs are brown and crisp. Turn ribs over occasionally.

Short Ribs

Mix together flour, paprika, salt and pepper. Pat beef ribs dry with absorbent paper and rub with spice mixture.

Heat the oil in a frying pan and brown the beef ribs well. Transfer to the slow cooker.

Add a little more oil to frying pan, if necessary, and sauté onion until golden brown. Pour contents of pan into slow cooker, add the carrot and stock and stir.

Combine the purée and gently mix through meat and vegetables in slow cooker. Cook for 6–8 hours on low or 5–6 hours on high. Adjust seasoning if necessary, and if tomato mixture is a little sharp, add sugar. Allow dish to cool, remove all fat, and reheat to serve.

2 tablespoons plain (all-purpose) flour

1 tablespoon sweet paprika

salt and freshly ground black pepper

1½ lb (750g) short beef ribs

1 tablespoon vegetable oil

3 onions, sliced

1 carrot, sliced

2 tablespoons beef stock

1 cup tomato purée

1 teaspoon sugar (optional)

Glazed Steak with Porcini Sauce

SERVES 4

4 rib eye steaks
3½oz (100g) dried porcini
mushrooms
10½oz (300g) fresh mushrooms,
sliced
1 tablespoon olive oil
⅔oz (20g) unsalted butter
1 tablespoon light soy sauce
1 tablespoon white miso paste

Trim steaks of any unwanted fat.

Place the dried mushrooms in a bowl with a cup of boiling water, let stand for 30 minutes to rehydrate. Retain liquid.

In a medium-size saucepan over a medium heat, cook the fresh mushrooms with the olive oil and butter for 3 minutes, stirring occasionally. Carefully add the porcini mushrooms and liquid, then the soy sauce and miso and stir to combine.

Simmer for 10 minutes, or until the liquid has reduced to a sauce consistency, and keep warm.

Preheat the barbecue to high. Drizzle the steaks with some of the mushroom sauce and cook steaks on the barbecue for 2–3 minutes on each side. Reduce heat to medium, brush steaks with more mushroom sauce and cook until meat is done to your liking. Serve steaks with mashed potato in winter or a fresh garden salad in summer.

Drunken Sirloin Steaks

Trim steaks of any visible fat. Place beer, garlic, Worcestershire sauce and tomato sauce in a large shallow ceramic or glass dish and mix to combine.

Add steaks to marinade, turn to coat, cover and set aside to marinate at room temperature for at least 3 hours, or in the refrigerator overnight. Turn occasionally during marinating.

Preheat the barbecue to hot. Drain steaks and reserve marinade. Cook steaks on lightly oiled barbecue, brushing with reserved marinade, for 3–5 minutes each side or until cooked to your liking. Serve immediately.

4 bone-in sirloin steaks
DRUNKEN MARINADE
6fl oz (180ml) beer
2 cloves garlic, crushed
2fl oz (60ml) Worcestershire sauce
2fl oz (60ml) tomato sauce
oil for cooking

Marinated BBQ Steak with Chimichurri

SERVES 4

4 sirloin steaks
3 red onions, cut into wedges
3 tomatoes, cut into wedges
2fl oz (60ml) olive oil
2fl oz (60ml) red wine vinegar
1 teaspoon dried oregano
1 teaspoon sweet paprika
salt and freshly ground black
  pepper
chimichurri sauce, to serve

Place steaks, onions and tomatoes in a large shallow ceramic dish.

Combine olive oil, red wine vinegar, dried oregano, sweet paprika, salt and pepper in a jug. Pour over steaks, onions and tomatoes cover with plastic wrap and place in the fridge to marinate for 30 minutes. Remove steaks from marinade.

Cook steaks, onions and tomatoes on a barbecue plate or grill for 3 minutes each side or until cook to your liking.

Serve steaks with onion wedges, tomato wedges, chimichurri sauce and salad.

Oxtail and Tomato Soup

SERVES **6**

Have the oxtail cut into sections by your butcher and place it in a boiling pot with the onion, carrot, celery and beef stock.

Simmer until the meat is cooked and is leaving the bone. Remove from the heat and lift the oxtail out. Reserve the stock. Cool the meat and then remove it from the bone. Dice finely and return it to the reserved stock.

Add the tomato, rosemary, salt and pepper. Bring to the boil and cook for 10 minutes. Check the seasoning and serve with crusty bread.

1 medium oxtail
1 medium onion, chopped
1 large carrot, sliced
1 stalk celery, diced
8 cups beef stock
2 tomatoes, peeled, deseeded and chopped
salt and freshly ground black pepper
1 sprig rosemary, leaves removed and chopped

Oxtail Soup

1 oxtail
1 tablespoon seasoned flour
2 tablespoons oil
6 cups beef stock
1 carrot, sliced
1 small turnip, sliced
1 onion, roughly chopped
2 stalks celery, chopped
2–3 bay leaves
salt
pinch of cayenne pepper
juice of 1 lemon
1 teaspoon Worcestershire sauce
3 tablespoons sherry or Madeira

Coat oxtail in seasoned flour. Heat oil over a medium heat, add oxtail and cook until brown. Add stock and simmer for 2 hours. Skim off the froth.

Place vegetables and bay leaves in the stock and cook for a further 15–20 minutes.

Remove meat from bones, return the meat to soup and reheat. Season with salt and cayenne pepper. Stir in lemon juice and Worcestershire sauce. Just before serving, add sherry.

Oxtail with Black Olives

Heat a medium non-stick frying pan over high heat. Add oxtail and cook for 2 minutes or until browned.

Place oxtail in a slow cooker, add wine and brandy, then cover and cook on high for 30 minutes to bring oxtail to temperature.

Add stock, rosemary, orange rind and garlic. Season with salt and freshly ground pepper. Cover and cook for 8 hours on low.

Add the olives and cook for a further hour. You may want to reduce the sauce further by straining it into a small saucepan and rapidly boiling it for 5 minutes or until sauce has thickened. Serve on a bed of steamed rice.

NOTE
Ask your butcher to cut the oxtail into joints.

2 small or 1 large oxtail, trimmed of fat
¼ cup dry white wine
⅓ cup brandy
1½ cups hot beef stock
3 sprigs fresh rosemary
grated rind of 1 orange
2 cloves garlic, crushed
salt and freshly ground black pepper
1 cup pitted black olives

Portuguese Steak with Onions

2fl oz (60ml) red wine vinegar

2 cloves garlic, crushed

1 teaspoon ground sweet paprika

salt and freshly ground black
  pepper

4 medium sirloin steaks

2fl oz (60ml) olive oil

2 onions, roughly chopped

4 tomatoes, diced

2 bay leaves, halved

2fl oz (60ml) red wine

2 tablespoons continental
  parsley, freshly chopped

Mix together 2 tablespoons red wine vinegar, garlic, paprika, salt and pepper. Rub the mixture evenly over the steaks.

Heat 1 tablespoon oil in a frying pan over medium heat. Add onions and cook until golden. Add tomatoes, bay leaves and red wine. Cook for 5–10 minutes or until mixture has reduced. Stir through remaining red wine vinegar and parsley.

Meanwhile in another frying pan, heat remaining oil over medium to high heat. Add steaks and cook for 2–3 minutes each side or until cooked to your liking.

Spoon tomato mixture over steaks and serve with chips.

Salsa Rib Roast

Preheat oven to 400°F (200°C). Rub the roast with salt, pepper and crushed garlic. Just before placing in the oven, dust all over with flour—this helps to seal in the juices. Place in the oven and cook for 50 minutes until medium rare (cook for a further 15 minutes for well done).

Meanwhile, combine all salsa ingredients in a small saucepan ready for heating. Remove the roast from the oven and rest the meat for 5 minutes. Warm the salsa while the meat rests.

6-point standing rib roast of beef, about 3lb 5oz (1½kg)
salt and freshly ground black pepper
2 cloves garlic, crushed
2 tablespoons all-purpose (plain) flour
TOMATO SALSA
8 Roma tomatoes, finely chopped
1 medium red onion, finely chopped
10 leaves basil, chopped
sprinkle of garlic bread seasoning salt
1 tablespoon olive oil
1½ tablespoons balsamic dressing

Veal

Veal

PAN-FRYING VEAL

Points for success

* Season veal with pepper and herbs before frying. Add salt after cooking. As veal is mild in flavour, extra flavour can be added by:

* Cutting a large clove of garlic in half and rubbing cut surface over veal to give a faint garlic flavour.

* Sprinkling veal with lemon juice and pepper five minutes before pan frying.

* Placing veal in a marinade before frying.

* Use a wide heavy-based pan that will accommodate the veal in one layer. If many pieces are to be cooked, keep the first batch hot by placing on a plate over a pan of simmering water, cover with a lid, overturned plate or foil.

* Serve pan-fried veal as soon as it is cooked.

* Thin veal steaks need only 1–2 minutes cooking on each side, depending on thickness. Overcooking will toughen the veal.

* Deglaze frying pan after cooking veal with stock, wine or fruit juices, to make a tasty sauce.

* For best results, use a mixture of oil and butter for pan-frying veal. Ghee is also suitable—it gives a good flavour and will not burn.

* Heat butter and oil well before adding veal steaks. The steaks should sizzle as soon as they hit the pan.

* Make sure that veal steaks are of even thickness. If not, flatten them out by placing between two pieces of baking paper and lightly pound them with a meat mallet or rolling pin. Snip edges in places to prevent curling during cooking.

* Boned shoulder and leg roasts are best stuffed. Use a moist stuffing.

* Place veal fat-side down for first half of cooking time, then turn.

* Veal needs to be well cooked—rare veal is unpalatable, and if cooked to well done there is a danger of toughening. Aim for something between medium and well done. Cook for 30 minutes per 17½oz (500g). If the roast is very thick, cook for 35 minutes per 17½oz (500g). To test if done, pierce meat at thickest part with a skewer—if juices run clear, the veal is cooked. If juices are pink, return to oven.

* Baste veal with pan juices during cooking.

* Rest roast for 10–15 minutes before carving.

* Always remember to deglaze the roasting pan with a little liquid, scraping up every speck of brown sediment—this is where the flavour for the gravy comes from.

* Being a comparatively delicate meat, veal benefits from cooking in an oven bag. Moisture is retained and the baked result is tender and delicious.

GRILLING VEAL

Points for success

* Marinate the veal in an oil-based marinade—the oil prevents the veal from drying out. Extra flavour is also added to the meat. Brush with marinade during cooking.

* Best results are obtained with thicker cuts of veal.

* If thin veal steaks are to be grilled, marinate then cook for 1½–2 minutes on each side.

* If no marinade is being used, brush veal with oil before and during cooking to keep it moist and tender.

* For extra flavour, brush veal with onion or garlic juice before grilling. Add salt and pepper when placing under grill.

* Have grill pan cold before placing meat on it. It is best to line grill pan with foil before grilling to catch the meat juices. Pour juices over veal when serving. Cooking in its juices will also keep the veal moist and tender.

* Prepare all accompaniments before commencing to grill.

* Marinated veal may be barbecued, particularly skewered veal. Use the same recipes as for grilling. However, the fiercer heat source and the closeness to the heat may overcook the veal and toughen it. Place a rack on the barbecue plate and place meat on the rack. This takes it off direct heat.

Baked Veal Cutlets with Gremolata

Combine the rice with 2 cups water in a saucepan. Bring to the boil, reduce heat to low, cover and cook for 15 minutes. Remove from heat, allow to stand covered for 10 minutes.

Meanwhile preheat oven to 400°F (200°C). Place tomatoes on a baking tray, drizzle with half the olive oil and bake for 10 minutes. Stir tomatoes and chives through rice. Set aside and keep warm.

Heat a little oil in a heavy-based frying pan and sear the cutlets quickly on both sides. Remove and arrange in a shallow baking dish.

In a small bowl, combine the remaining olive oil, the lemon juice and zest, honey and mustard. Pour over veal and season. Bake for 5–8 minutes or until cooked to your liking. Allow meat to rest for 5 minutes before serving.

Combine gremolata ingredients, scatter over veal and serve on the rice.

1 cup long-grain rice
9oz (250g) cherry tomatoes
2 tablespoons olive oil
1 small bunch chives, finely chopped
4 veal cutlets
juice and zest of 1 lemon
1 teaspoon honey
1 tablespoon Dijon mustard
salt and freshly ground black pepper
GREMOLATA
zest of 2 lemons
¼ cup fresh parsley, finely chopped
2 cloves garlic, finely chopped

Marinated Veal Cutlets

4 veal cutlets

¼ cup olive oil

¼ cup white wine vinegar

2 tablespoons lemon juice

2 cloves garlic, crushed

2 bay leaves, crumbled

2 red chillies, deseeded and finely
  chopped

¼ cup freshly flat-leaf parsley,
  chopped

¼ cup freshly cilantro
  (coriander), chopped

salt and freshly ground black
  pepper

2 red onions, cut into quarters

4 Roma tomatoes, halved

½ bunch watercress, trimmed

Place veal in a large ceramic dish. Mix together olive oil, white wine vinegar, lemon juice, garlic, bay leaves, chillies, parsley, coriander, salt and pepper.

Pour marinade over veal, cover with cling wrap and place in the refrigerator for 2–3 hours to marinate.

Remove veal from marinade. Cook veal on a barbecue grill or plate for 3–4 minutes each side or until cooked, basting from time to time.

Cook onions and tomatoes on barbecue grill for 2–3 minutes each side or until cooked.

Serve veal cutlets with onions, tomatoes and watercress.

Creole Veal Chops

Place veal chops in a shallow ceramic dish. Combine ¼ cup olive oil, the lemon juice and zest, salt and pepper. Pour over chops and toss to combine. Cover with cling wrap and place in the refrigerator to marinate for 1–2 hours.

Heat 1 tablespoon olive oil in a large frying pan over medium heat. Remove veal from marinade, reserving marinade. Cook veal for 1–2 minutes each side or until brown. Remove and set aside.

Heat remaining oil over medium heat. Cook mushrooms for 1–2 minutes each side or until brown. Remove and set aside.

Add reserved marinade, garlic, half the oregano, the bay leaves, white wine, beef stock, French mustard and tomato paste. Bring to the boil. Return meat and mushrooms to the pan and reduce heat to low. Cover and simmer for 5–8 minutes or until veal is tender.

Top veal with mushrooms, spoon over sauce and garnish with remaining oregano. Serve with potatoes and green beans.

4 veal chops
½ cup olive oil
juice and finely grated zest of
* 1 lemon*
salt and freshly ground black
* pepper*
4 large Swiss or flat mushrooms
2 cloves garlic, crushed
¼ cup oregano, chopped
2 bay leaves
¼ cup white wine
½ cup beef stock
2 teaspoons French mustard
1 tablespoon tomato paste

Veal Osso Bucco

4 large veal shanks (osso bucco),
    about 5oz (150g) each
¼ cup seasoned flour
¼ cup olive oil
1 onion, finely chopped
1 clove garlic, crushed
¾ cup tomato pasta sauce
½ cup beef stock
14oz (400g) canned diced
    tomatoes
2 carrots, sliced
2 stalks celery, sliced
finely grated zest of 1 lemon, plus
    strips to garnish
14oz (400g) canned cannellini
    beans, drained
¼ cup fresh parsley, chopped

Coat the veal shanks lightly in seasoned flour. Heat 2 tablespoons oil in a large saucepan over medium–high heat. Brown the veal shanks, then remove and set aside. Heat the remaining oil, add the onion and garlic and cook for 2–3 minutes or until soft. Add the tomato pasta sauce, stock, tomatoes, carrots, celery and lemon zest. Return the veal to the pan.

Cover and simmer for 35–40 minutes or until tender. Add a little more stock if needed. Stir in the beans and parsley and cook until heated through. Garnish with extra lemon zest. Serve with mashed potatoes or polenta.

NOTE
If you have time, simmer the meat over low heat for as long as possible until the meat starts to fall off the bone.

Rack of Veal with Thyme

SERVES 4

Preheat the oven to 350°F (180°C).

Boil the potatoes until soft. Drain, then mash or purée, and add half the olive oil, the chopped capers and 1 tablespoon roasted garlic purée. Mix well, season with salt and pepper, and set aside until ready to serve.

Heat remaining olive oil in a pan and brown the veal on both sides, until well sealed (approximately 5 minutes). Remove the veal from the pan, and place on a rack in a baking dish. Rub with remaining roasted garlic purée and half the thyme, and season with salt and pepper. Add half the wine and stock to the baking dish.

Roast in the oven for 20 minutes, or until veal is cooked to your liking. Wrap in foil and let rest for 10 minutes.

Add remaining stock, wine and thyme to the pan juices and cook over a medium heat for 5 minutes, until the liquid has reduced by one-third.

Serve veal on the mashed potato with pan juices, and garnish with extra sprig of thyme.

1lb 10oz (750g) potatoes, peeled and cut into large dice
⅓ cup olive oil
1 tablespoon capers, chopped
2 tablespoons roasted garlic purée
salt and freshly ground black pepper
2lb 3oz (1kg) rack of veal (8 points)
8 sprigs thyme, leaves removed and stalks discarded
1¼ cups dry white wine
1¼ cups chicken stock

Lemon Pepper Veal Chops

SERVES 4–6

4–6 veal loin chops about 1in
  (2.5cm) thick
1½ tablespoons olive oil
1½ tablespoons lemon juice
2 teaspoons lemon pepper
8oz (250g) each potato and
  sweet potato, peeled, boiled and
  mashed with butter and milk
1½ teaspoons chopped fresh chilli
½ cup relish

Mix the oil, lemon juice and lemon pepper together. Pour into a suitable size non-metallic dish. Add the chops and coat on both sides. Cover and marinate for 2 hours or more in the refrigerator.

Prepare sweet potato mash, then stir in the chilli.

Prepare barbecue for direct-heat cooking. Arrange coals for direct two-zone heating. Arrange gas burners likewise.

Place the chops onto the hot, well-greased grill bars and sear well on both sides. Move to moderate part of the barbecue and continue to cook for about 3 minutes on each side to desired degree. Brush with the seasoning while cooking. Sit the sweet potato mash on barbecue to warm.

Top the chops with a good spoonful of relish and garnish with salad greens.

Honey-glazed Chops with Pineapple Rice

SERVES 4

Season chops with salt and pepper. Coat both sides with honey, then sprinkle with chilli powder, cover and refrigerate for 1 hour or more. Retain remaining marinade for glazing.

While chops are marinating, prepare the pineapple rice. Place stock and pineapple juice in a skillet, bring to the boil and stir in the rice. Cover and simmer for 15 minutes. Stir in the peas and scallions, cook 3 minutes more. Turn off the heat, stir through the pineapple pieces. Cover and set aside.

Prepare barbecue or hot plate for direct-heat cooking. Prepare coals for medium high; the same for gas cooking, turning heat to medium when cooking begins.

Place the chops on the barbecue and cook for 5 minutes, brush with marinade and turn. Cook for a few minutes more, brushing with marinade and turning until chops are cooked and well glazed.

Meanwhile, reheat the pineapple rice at the side of the grill plate. Serve chops on a bed of pineapple rice. Drizzle a little fresh marinade over rice if desired.

8 veal short loin chops, ¾in (1.5cm) thick
MARINADE
salt and pepper
¾ cup honey
½ teaspoon chilli powder
PINEAPPLE RICE
1 cup chicken bouillon
½ cup unsweetened pineapple juice
¾ cup jasmine rice
1 cup peas
½ cup scallions (spring onions), sliced
3 slices fresh pineapple, cored and cut into small dice

Veal Rib Roast with Shallots and Garlic

SERVES 6–8

3lb (1.5kg) standing rib roast of
veal

¾ cup red wine and garlic
marinade (see Chump Chops
with Garlic Mash)

17½oz (500g) shallots

2 whole heads of garlic

3 tablespoons vegetable oil mixed
with 2 tablespoons water

1½lb (750g) small chat potatoes,
washed

SHALLOT DRESSING

1 tablespoon olive oil, combined
with 1 teaspoon balsamic
vinegar

½ tablespoon fresh oregano

1 tablespoon fresh basil, finely
chopped

1 tablespoon fresh parsley, finely
chopped

salt to taste

1 tablespoon cracked black pepper

Place meat into a non-metallic dish. Cover and refrigerate for 2 to 3 hours. Stand at room temperature for 20 minutes before cooking.

While veal is standing, trim the root ends of the shallots. Place in a foil baking tray with the garlic heads. Place potatoes in second tray. Toss both with oil water mixture.

Prepare the barbecue for indirect-heat cooking, medium-high heat, and place a drip tray in the centre. Brush the veal with marinade. Place the shallot and potato trays over indirect heat at each end of the roast. Cover with lid or hood and cook for 40 minutes.

Open lid, move trays to direct heat at each side of the roast. Toss the shallots, turn the potatoes. When done, shallots and garlic should be very soft, potatoes tender and browned. Brush roast with marinade close lid and continue to cook 10 minutes.

Open lid, brush the roast with marinade. Test the shallots and potatoes and remove if or when ready. Continue to brush the roast with marinade every 8–10 minutes until cooking time of 65 minutes is completed.

Veal Cutlet Parmigiana

SERVES 4

Bring the cutlets to room temperature (about 15 minutes). Mix the oil, garlic and seasonings together and rub into the cutlets on both sides.

Mix the diced tomato, sugar, green onion and parsley together, add salt and pepper to taste and set aside.

Preheat the grill for 5 minutes then cover the bottom plate with a sheet of baking paper. Place the cutlets on top, close the grill and cook for 5 minutes.

Open the grill and spoon a pile of tomato mixture on top of each cutlet. Cover with a sheet of baking paper, close and cook until heated through (about 30 seconds). Open the grill and lift the baking paper. Top each cutlet with 1 tablespoon of grated mozzarella, replace the baking paper and cook for 10–15 seconds to melt the cheese. Remove the paper, then close the lid for 3 seconds to sear the cheese. Serve immediately.

4 veal cutlets, ⅓–½in (1–1½cm) thick
2 teaspoons olive oil
1 clove garlic, crushed
salt and pepper
2 Roma tomatoes, diced
½ teaspoon sugar
3 scallions (spring onions), finely sliced
1 tablespoon parsley, finely chopped
6 tablespoons mozzarella cheese, grated

Rustic Baked Veal

Preheat oven to 350°F (180°C) and line a lasagne dish with baking paper.

Place the chops in one layer onto the baking paper and cover with the sliced onions.

Combine the red wine, tomato paste, sugar, garlic and salt and pepper and pour over the chops. Tightly cover with aluminium foil and bake for 1 hour.

Serve with seasonal vegetables and garnish with chopped parsley.

8 thick veal chops

2 large sliced onions

½ cup red wine

1 tablespoon tomato paste

½ teaspoon sugar

2 cloves garlic, crushed

salt and pepper to taste

finely chopped parsley, to garnish

Pork

Pork

STORAGE

REFRIGERATION	Correct storage of pork, uncooked or cooked, is vital to avoid spoilage and waste. Fresh pre-packed meat obtained from your butcher can be stored in the refrigerator for up to 3 days.
FREEZING	If freezing pork, use ziplock bags, with a sheet of baking paper separating each piece of meat to prevent sticking and damage to meat fibres when thawing. Small cuts can be stored up to three months, larger cuts up to six months.
THAWING	When required, move pork from freezer to refrigerator and allow to thaw evenly overnight.
COOKED PORK	Cooked pork should be covered or wrapped in cling wrap and placed in the refrigerator at least 1 hour after cooking. It will keep perfectly for several days. It can also be frozen and stored for up to 1 month.

PAN-FRYING PORK

Points for success

* Use a heavy-based frying pan with just enough butter or oil to film the surface.
* Heat on a medium-high heat and add pork. Cook for 30 seconds to 1 minute on each side then lower heat to moderate and cook about 4 minutes on each side or until meat is springy to touch.
* If pork is crumbed, add oil or oil and butter to the pan to a depth of $1/8$in (3mm). Heat well, add pork and brown both sides on brisk heat, then lower the heat and cook a further 3–4 minutes on each side to cook through. The pan may be partially covered with a lid to keep the pork moist.
* Remove pork and add a liquid to cover base of pan. Stir residue to lift pan juices and make into a light gravy to serve with pork.

STIR-FRYING PORK

Points for success

* Suitable cuts: diced pork, leg, shoulder, foreloin roast cut into dice, loin, fillet or schnitzel cut into strips or thin squares.
* Partly freeze meat before cutting into strips to make it easier to slice. Slice across the grain in very thin slices.
* Marinate pork before stir-frying to add moisture and flavour.

BRAISING AND CASSEROLING PORK

Points for success

* Suitable cuts: diced pork, shoulder cuts, leg steaks, foreloin steaks, loin chops.
* Pork may be browned first in butter or oil before the liquid is added. Brown on moderate heat. Dust pork with seasoned flour before browning to keep juices in.
* Use a heavy-based saucepan or a lidded frying pan for stovetop cooking, a covered casserole for oven cooking.
* Always cook at a slow simmer, on low heat. Never bring to the boil, it will toughen.
* Add enough liquid to come halfway up the side of the meat.

ROASTING PORK

Points for success

* Always weigh roast to calculate cooking time. Allow approximately 30 minutes per 17½oz (500g) of boneless pork, plus an extra 30 minutes for thick roasts.
* To cook pork perfectly, use a meat thermometer. The internal temperature should reach 170°F (76°C).
* Remove the rind from the roast and cook it separately. This will considerably reduce fat content of the roast and will give a crisp, crunchy crackle. When the roast has cooked, remove from oven and turn oven to high to crisp the crackling.
* To test if cooked, pierce thickest part of pork with a skewer—if juices run clear, pork is done. Rindless pork may be cooked in an oven bag. It shortens the cooking time and gives a moist result.
* Allow 10 minutes standing time prior to carving, otherwise juices will escape and pork will lose its tenderness.
* Many interesting flavours can be added to pork in a marinade, topping or stuffing—fruit and fruit juice flavours, dried fruits, herbs, ginger and honey are all suitable.

GRILLING PORK

Points for success

* Remove rind from pork if not already removed. If you wish to cook it, cook separately under hot griller.
* Always cook pork under a medium heat. High heat will dry it out and make the pork tough.
* Grill pork approximately 5 minutes each side, according to thickness. To retain moisture, brush pork with a marinade or a little oil before and during cooking.
* Season pork with pepper and herbs before grilling. Salt may be sprinkled on during cooking.
* Pork will benefit by marinating in an oil-based marinade for 20 minutes before grilling. As well as retaining moisture, flavour will also be added.
* Remember to slash the selvedge to prevent curling.
* Grilled pork must be served immediately.

BARBECUING PORK

Points for success

* Choose a thick chop or steak—thin cuts tend to dry out. Leg steaks and forequarter chops are ideal.
* Marinate pork for at least 30 minutes to keep pork moist and add flavour.
* Trim off excess fat and the rind. Fat drips into the coals and creates flames and smoke.Cook over medium heat, not hot, as pork will dry out and toughen.
* For kebabs and skewered pork, it is advisable to place on a wire rack which stands $1/3$in (1cm) off the plate. The direct heat is too fierce for the small cubes.

Teriyaki Pork Short Ribs

SERVES **4**

Cut ribs into 2in (5cm) pieces. Sprinkle with salt and pepper. Heat oil in a frying pan and sear ribs until brown, about 10–15 minutes.

Remove ribs and set aside. Add onions, carrots, celery, fennel, lemongrass, garlic and ginger to frying pan and sauté until soft.

Add teriyaki sauce, rice wine, soy sauce, thyme and bay leaves. Transfer vegetables into a large saucepan. Return ribs to the vegetable mixture and add 2 cups water.

Bring to the boil and then reduce heat to simmer. Cover and cook for 3 hours or until ribs are very tender. Remove ribs and set aside.

Reduce liquid by a third, then discard the lemongrass, thyme and bay leaves. Pour the sauce over the ribs and serve with steamed rice.

12 pork ribs

2 teaspoons salt

2 teaspoons freshly ground black pepper

2 tablespoons canola oil

5 large onions, roughly chopped

3 carrots, roughly chopped

3 stalks celery, roughly chopped

2 medium fennel bulbs, roughly chopped

4 stalks lemongrass, bruised

5 cloves garlic, minced

1½in (4cm) piece ginger, grated

1 cup teriyaki sauce

2 cups Chinese rice wine

1½ cups dark soy sauce

6 sprigs fresh thyme

3 bay leaves

Pork Spare Ribs on Sourdough

3lb (1.5kg) pork spare ribs
1 cup barbecue sauce
1 round loaf sourdough bread
1 cup mango chutney
GARLIC BUTTER
6oz (170g) salted butter at room
  temperature
4 teaspoons freshly crushed garlic
½ teaspoon lemon pepper

Sprinkle each spare rib lightly on both sides with meat tenderiser. Stand at room temperature for 20 minutes. Cut sourdough bread into ¾in (1.5cm) thick slices. Halve the larger centre slices. Mix garlic butter ingredients together and spread on both sides of the bread. Take a small bowl, a brush, barbecue sauce and chutney to barbecue area.

Prepare barbecue for direct-heat cooking on high. Oil the grill bars or plate well. Brush the ribs lightly on both sides with the barbecue sauce and place on the hottest part of the grill. Sear for 2–3 minutes on each side.

Brush top of ribs with the sauce and turn sauce side down onto the grill. Cook for 8 minutes then brush the top side with sauce and turn. Cook for 8 minutes more. Brush once more and turn and cook for 2 minutes. Repeat and cook until done to your liking.

During last stage of cooking place the garlic bread onto the grill. Cook to toast both sides. To serve, place a rib onto each bread slice and top with chutney. Serve immediately.

Smoky Barbecue Spare Ribs

SERVES 6–8

Place the ribs in a large, non-metallic dish. Thoroughly combine relish and the oil and liberally brush relish onto ribs. Cover and marinate in refrigerator for several hours or overnight, turning occasionally.

Take 2 large sheets of heavy-duty foil and place on a work surface. Place a rack of ribs on each. Generously cover both sides of ribs with extra marinade. Wrap into a double-folded parcel, making sure all joins are well sealed to prevent leakage. Carefully place parcel onto a tray, taking care not to tear the foil. Refrigerate if not cooking immediately.

Prepare the barbecue for direct-heat cooking. Place a wire cake rack on the grill bars to stand 1in (2.5cm) above grill. Place the foil parcels on the rack and cook for 10 minutes on each side for a total of 20 minutes.

Remove to a plate. Open foil and discard. Lift ribs onto the rack. Continue cooking and brush with extra relish, turning until ribs are well browned and crisp, for about 10 minutes. Cut between the ribs, pile onto a platter and serve immediately.

2 x 2lb (1kg) racks American-style ribs
¾ cup store-bought smoky barbecue marinade
¼ cup olive oil

Marinated Pork T-bone Steak

SERVES 4

4–6 thick pork loin chops
⅓ cup olive oil
¼ cup soy sauce
1 teaspoon freshly chopped ginger
2 teaspoons French mustard
¼ teaspoon cracked black pepper
wholegrain mustard
mayonnaise
2 oranges, unpeeled, thinly sliced
watercress sprigs

In a small bowl, mix the oil, soy sauce, ginger, mustard and pepper together. Rub the mixture well into both sides of the chops, and then place in a shallow dish. Cover and marinate 4 hours or more in the refrigerator. Reserve remaining marinade. Prepare garnish. Take all to the barbecue area.

Prepare barbecue for direct-heat cooking to high heat. Oil the grill bars well. Place on the chops. Cook for 7–8 minutes each side or until cooked through. Turn the chops once and brush occasionally with marinade.

Grill the orange slices 1 minute on each side, brushing lightly with marinade. Remove chops to a warmed platter and spoon a little sauce along centre of chops. Top with a drizzle of mayonnaise. Garnish with the orange and watercress. Serve remaining sauce in a sauce jug.

Honey Citrus Thick Loin Chops

SERVES 4–6

Wipe over the chops with clean kitchen towel, trim off fat. Mix the marinade ingredients Brush half of the marinade onto both sides of the chops. Stand for 20 minutes at room temperature, or longer in the refrigerator, before cooking. Scrub the potatoes and wrap each in foil, while marinating chops.

Prepare barbecue for indirect-heat cooking, Insert a drip tray. Heat charcoal to medium high; gas to high and turn to medium when food is placed on.

Place the chops on the well-oiled grill bars over the drip tray. Place the potatoes in a foil tray and stand over direct heat. Close lid and cook for 7 minutes.

Open hood. Test and turn the potatoes and brush the chops with marinade. Cook for 7 minutes more.

Remove potatoes, brush chops with marinade and turn. Close hood, cook chops for 5 minutes. Test to determine further cooking time. Brush regularly with marinade and cook until done to your liking. Remove chops, cover and rest for 5 minutes.

Place the lemon halves over direct heat, brush with marinade. Cook for 2 minutes each side while brushing with marinade until golden and skin is soft.

Unwrap potatoes and cut in half. Brush with garlic butter. Serve the chops with the grilled Kipfler potatoes and lemon.

6 thick-cut pork loin chops
1 lemon, halved
MARINADE
2 tablespoons honey
1 tablespoon orange zest
¼ cup orange juice
1½ tablespoons soy sauce
1½ tablespoons Dijon mustard
2 teaspoons freshly crushed garlic
1 teaspoon freshly chopped ginger
POTATOES
3lb (1.5kg) medium-sized Kipfler
  potatoes
2 tablespoons butter
1 teaspoon crushed garlic

Pork Cutlets with Quince

1 tablespoon olive oil

4 pork cutlets

SAUCE

⅔fl oz (20ml) olive oil

1 clove garlic, crushed

1 medium red onion, sliced

1 medium quince, peeled, cored
  and cut into thin wedges

½ cup white wine

juice of 1 orange (2½fl oz/75mL)

½ cup chicken stock

cinnamon stick

1 tablespoon honey

1 tablespoon parsley, chopped

salt and freshly ground pepper

Heat one tablespoon of oil in a large frying pan.

Add pork and brown quickly for 2–3 minutes on each side. Set meat aside.

Heat extra oil in pan. Add garlic and onion, and cook for 2–3 minutes. Add quince and cook for a further 3 minutes. Add white wine and cook for 2 minutes (or until reduced).

Stir in orange juice, chicken stock, cinnamon stick and honey, and cook on a low heat for 10–15 minutes (or until sauce has thickened slightly). Return meat to the pan, and cook for a further 5–10 minutes. Stir in the parsley, salt and pepper, spoon over the cutlets, and serve.

Sparerib Chops with Red Cabbage and Apples

SERVES 4

Preheat the oven to 350°F (180°C). Heat the oil in a large flameproof casserole dish. Add the spare rib chops and cook for 1½–2 minutes on each side, until lightly browned. Remove and keep warm. Add the onion and cook for another 5 minutes or until softened and golden.

Sir in the cabbage, apples and wine or stock. Season to taste.Place the pork chops on top and cover tightly. Cook in the oven for 1¼–1½ hours, until the pork is tender (you may need to add a little more wine or stock during cooking if the dish starts to dry out). Serve garnished with the parsley.

NOTE

The sweet and sour flavour of red cabbage and apples is perfect with pork. Make sure you buy the meatier spare rib chops and not plain ribs. Serve with mashed potatoes.

2 tablespoons vegetable oil
4 large pork spare rib chops
1 onion, chopped
17½oz (500g) red cabbage, finely shredded
17½oz (500g) cooking apples, peeled, cored and thinly sliced
1 cup red wine or vegetable stock
salt and black pepper
fresh Italian parsley to garnish

Pan-fried Pork Steaks with Orange and Sage

SERVES 4

1 tablespoon olive oil

salt and black pepper

12 thin-cut pork loin steaks

1 1/5 cups chicken stock

finely grated zest and juice of
*   1 orange*

2 tablespoons dry sherry or
*   vermouth*

2 tablespoons redcurrant jelly

2 teaspoons chopped fresh sage or
*   1 teaspoon dried sage*

Heat the oil in a large heavy-based frying pan. Season the steaks. Add 6 steaks to the pan and fry for 4 minutes each side or until cooked. Remove from the pan and keep warm while you fry the rest of the steaks. Add to the first batch and keep warm.

Add the stock, orange zest and juice, sherry or vermouth and redcurrant jelly to the pan. Cook vigorously over a high heat for 5 minutes, stirring, or until reduced by half and darkened in colour.

Stir the sage into the sauce and season with pepper and salt to taste. Return the steaks to the pan and heat for 1–2 minutes to warm through. Spoon over the sauce.

NOTE

Orange cuts through the richness of the pork in this quick and simple dish. Serve on a bed of shredded cabbage with new potatoes.

Glazed Pork Spare Ribs

Place the spare ribs on a large sheet of heavy-duty foil and cover both sides generously with the marinade. Wrap into a double-folded parcel, making sure all joins are well sealed to prevent leakage. Stand for at least 30 minutes before cooking. Place in the refrigerator if not being cooked immediately.

Prepare the barbecue for direct-heat cooking. Place a wire cake rack on the grill bars to stand 1in (2½cm) above the bars. Place the ribs in the foil parcel on the rack and cook for 10 minutes on each side.

Remove to a plate, remove the ribs and discard the foil, then return the ribs to the rack. Continue cooking, brushing with fresh marinade and turning each minute until the ribs are well browned and crisp (about 10 minutes). The total cooking time is approximately 30–35 minutes.

NOTE
Ribs may be cooked by indirect heat in a hooded barbecue. There is no need to wrap the ribs in foil.

Place over indirect heat after marinating. Brush and turn frequently with the lid down for 1 hour or more. Cooking in foil over direct heat cuts cooking time in half.

36oz (1kg) pork spare ribs (American-style)
soy and honey marinade (see Honey-glazed Spareribs)

Pork Chops, Chilli Rice and Glazed Apples

SERVES 6

6 pork loin chops ½in (1½cm)
   thick
salt and pepper
1 cup soy and honey marinade
   (see Honey-glazed Spareribs)
2 large apples, cored and cut into
   thick rings
2 teaspoons chilli powder
3 cups cooked rice

Trim fat from the chops as desired and sprinkle lightly with salt and pepper.

Heat the barbecue until hot and oil the grill bars. Place the chops on the grill and sear 1 side for 1 minute, turn and brush with marinade to glaze. Continue to turn at 2 minute intervals 4–5 times more until cooked to required degree. Take care not to overcook. Cooking time is 10–15 minutes depending on the thickness of the chops and the type of barbecue used.

Place the apple rings on the grill bars a little after the chops commence cooking. Turn 2–3 times until soft and glazed. Place a piece of baking paper under the apples to prevent scorching. If cooking on a charcoal barbecue, use foil which has been brushed with oil.

Mix the chilli and cooked rice together and heat on the side of the barbecue in a foil or metal dish. Serve the chops with the chilli rice and garnish with the glazed apple rings.

Pork Chops with Pistachio Sauce

To make pesto, combine pistachio nuts, garlic, arugula and olive oil in a food processor; blend to form a coarse paste.

Cook pork chops on a lightly oiled BBQ or grill on medium-high heat for 4–6 minutes each side (depending on thickness). Allow pork to rest for a few minutes before serving with pesto.

Serve with sweet potato wedges.

4–6 pork loin chops, fat trimmed

3½oz (100g) shelled pistachio nuts

1 clove garlic, peeled

½ cup well-packed fresh arugula (rocket) leaves

4½ tablespoons extra virgin olive oil

Teriyaki Pork Steaks

SERVES 4

4 pork loin steaks
1 cup teriyaki marinade
3½oz (100g) snow peas
1 red bell pepper (capsicum), cut
    into ¾in (2cm) pieces
1 yellow bell pepper (capsicum),
    cut into ¾in (2cm) pieces
1 small bunch scallions (spring
    onions), sliced into 1¼in (3cm)
    lengths
watercress to garnish
TERIYAKI MARINADE
½ cup soy sauce
½ cup orange juice
½ cup brown sugar
2 teaspoons ground ginger
3 cloves garlic, crushed

Place the steaks into a shallow dish and pour over ½ cup of the marinade to cover the steaks well. Cover and place into refrigerator for a few hours or over night.

Prepare the barbecue for direct heat cooking. Oil the grill well. Heat until hot. Place the pork steaks on the grill. Cook for 5–7 minutes on each side, brushing with extra marinade while they are cooking.

Brush all the vegetables with some of the marinade and cook on the grill until they are coloured and tender.

Place each steak onto a dinner plate and top with the cooked vegetables. Garnish with the watercress.
To make the teriyaki marinade, combine all ingredients in a glass bowl and stir well. Soak meat for at least 2 hours, covered in the refrigerator. Marinade can be used for brushing over meat while cooking.

Bak Siou

To make the paste, make the tamarind liquid by soaking 3 teaspoons tamarind pulp in 2½ tablespoons hot water. Stir and strain it when cool.

Toast the coriander in a dry wok or pan over low heat until aromatic.

Place all of the paste ingredients in a blender and blend until smooth.

Heat a wok or large pot over medium-low heat and add the oil. Fry the paste for 4 minutes, stirring frequently.

Add the ribs and stir well to coat with paste.

Add the water, bring to the boil, reduce heat, cover and simmer for 1 hour. Uncover and simmer for another 30 minutes until the pork is tender, stirring occasionally.

Serve with plain rice.

1 tablespoon vegetable oil
24oz (750g) pork spare ribs, cut into 2in (5cm) pieces
2 cups water
CORIANDER AND VINEGAR PASTE
2 tablespoons tamarind liquid
2 tablespoons ground coriander
¼ cup white vinegar
¼ cup scallions (spring onions) segments, roughly chopped
1 tablespoon palm sugar
¼ teaspoon salt

Honey-glazed Spareribs

SERVES 8

4lb 6oz (2kg) pork spareribs,
  trimmed of excess fat

2 onions, chopped

2 tablespoons fresh parsley,
  chopped

1 cup chicken stock

2 tablespoons lemon juice

4oz (125g) butter, melted

SOY-HONEY MARINADE

4 small fresh red chillies, chopped

4 cloves garlic, chopped

2 scallions (spring onions),
  chopped

1 tablespoon fresh ginger, finely
  grated

1½ cup rice-wine vinegar

½ cup soy sauce

6oz (170g) honey

To make marinade, combine chillies, garlic, scallions, ginger, vinegar, soy sauce and honey in a non-metallic dish. Add ribs, toss to coat, cover and marinate in the refrigerator for at least 4 hours.

Drain ribs and reserve marinade. Cook ribs, basting occasionally with reserved marinade, on a hot barbecue grill for 8–10 minutes or until ribs are tender and golden. Place on a serving platter, cover and keep warm.

Place remaining marinade in a saucepan, add onions, parsley, stock and lemon juice and bring to the boil. Reduce heat and simmer for 15 minutes or until sauce reduces by half. Pour mixture into a food processor or blender and process to make a purée. With motor running, pour in hot melted butter and process to combine. Serve sauce with spareribs.

Indonesian Spare Ribs

Pound the paste ingredients in a mortar and pestle or combine in a small food processor.

Chop spare ribs in half. Heat 1 tablespoon of oil in a wok or medium frying pan. Add spare ribs in 2 batches and fry for 2–3 minutes or until ribs are golden and crisp. Remove and set aside.

Heat remaining oil and add paste. Cook for 2 minutes, stirring constantly. Add coriander, cumin, black pepper, soy sauce, tamarind and sugar.

Turn all ingredients out into slow cooker set on a high heat setting. Return ribs to sauce, add water and cook for 4 hours, basting and turning every hour. Add a little extra water if sauce becomes too thick. Serve with Chinese greens and a side bowl of rice.

750g/1½ lb pork spare ribs
1½ tablespoons peanut oil
1 teaspoon ground coriander
½ teaspoon ground cumin
½ teaspoon freshly ground black
  pepper
2 tablespoons soy sauce
1 tablespoon tamarind
  concentrate
1 teaspoon brown sugar
¼ cup water
PASTE
2 French shallots, chopped
2 cloves garlic
2 teaspoons finely grated fresh
  ginger
¼ cup water

Pork Spare Ribs with Plum Sauce

2 racks baby back ribs, cut
   individually
½ cup plum jam
2 chicken stock cubes, crumbled
2 teaspoons cornstarch
   (cornflour)
3 teaspoons soy sauce
2 tablespoons dry sherry
1 clove minced garlic

Mix all of the ingredients together with 4 cups water and make sure each of the ribs is well coated with the marinade.

   Place in slow cooker and cook on low for 4 hours or high for 2–3 hours.

Spiced Spare Ribs

SERVES 4

Ask the butcher to chop spare ribs into 2in (5cm) pieces or use a sharp cleaver. Reserve. In a wok or heavy deep pan, stir-fry peppercorns with salt for about 5 minutes, stirring until salt colours. Remove. Then with mortar and pestle pound down peppercorns with five spice powder added.

Combine marinade ingredients and set aside. Rub half of the spice mix into spare ribs with your hands, add marinade and turn each rib to ensure each is fully coated. Marinate for at least 3 hours, preferably overnight.

Drain marinade from ribs and coat each rib with cornflour. Add more oil to wok until half full. Deep-fry ribs in batches over medium heat for about 4 minutes, remove, then re-fry until crisp and deeply golden.

Drain ribs. Place on warmed serving dish, sprinkle with remaining spice mix and serve garnished with parsley or cilantro.

36oz (1kg) meaty pork spare ribs
1 teaspoon Szechuan peppercorns
2 tablespoons cooking salt
½ teaspoon five spice powder
1½ tablespoons cornstarch
  (cornflour)
oil for deep-frying
parsley or cilantro (coriander)
  leaves
MARINADE
2½ tablespoons light soy sauce
2 teaspoons superfine
  (caster) sugar
2 tablespoons dry sherry
black pepper, freshly ground

Sweet Curried Pork Spareribs

SERVES 4

1kg (2lb) American-style pork
   ribs
3 tablespoons soy sauce
1 tablespoon honey
1 tablespoon brown vinegar
2 teaspoons curry paste
3 tablespoons tomato sauce
1 tablespoon sherry
2 cloves garlic, crushed
1 tablespoon grated fresh ginger
2 tablespoons chopped parsley
2 tablespoons sweet chilli sauce

Cut pork ribs into serving pieces (3–4 ribs per serve) and place into a large, non-metallic container. In a bowl, mix together soy sauce, honey, vinegar, curry paste, tomato sauce, sherry, garlic, ginger, parsley and sweet chilli sauce. Pour over the ribs. Cover and marinate for 3 hours or overnight in the refrigerator. Turn in marinade occasionally.

Preheat oven to 350°F (180°C). Remove ribs from marinade and place in a baking tray. Cook for 30–40 minutes, turning and brushing with marinade at 10 minute intervals. Serve immediately.

Honey-glazed Pork with Apple

Place pork cutlets on a flat platter. Brush each side with the marinade. Stand for 30 minutes before cooking.

Cut the apple into 12 to 16 wedges depending on size of apple.

Heat the barbecue grill to hot. Spray well with oil spray. Place on the chops and cook 4 minutes each side or to your liking, brushing with marinade as they cook.

Place on the apple wedges, turn to sear on both sides. Brush with marinade and turn frequently until tender and well glazed. Toss the rocket with dressing. Serve the chops on a bed of rocket leaves and pile apple wedges on top.

4 pork loin cutlets
6oz (175g) store-bought honey, garlic and soy marinade
2 large firm red apples
1 bunch rocket leaves
Italian dressing

Apple Pork Chops

2 tablespoons olive oil

6 pork loin chops, trimmed of fat

salt

6 green apples, cored and thickly
   sliced

1 tablespoon lemon juice

¼ cup brown sugar

¼ cup dried currants

Pour half the olive oil in a heavy-based frying pan and brown chops. Sprinkle with salt during browning.

Place into slow cooker, combine remaining ingredients and pour over the chops.

Cover and cook on low for 6–9 hours. The apples will break down to form most of the sauce and the meat will come away from the bone easily.

Grilled Pork Chops with Baked Sweet Potato

Preheat oven to 350°F (180°C).

Marinate chops in Worcestershire sauce and garlic for two hours.

Bake sweet potato at 350°F (180°C) for an hour.

Grill the chops on both sides until cooked so there is no pink in the middle.

Cut sweet potato with a sharp knife before serving.

Sweet potatoes can be topped with butter and salt and pepper; butter and lemon pepper; or butter with brown sugar and cinnamon.

2 teaspoons minced garlic

4 tablespoons Worcestershire sauce

2 pork chops (chops that are 1in/2½cm thick)

BAKED SWEET POTATO

2 sweet potatoes

salt, pepper, lemon pepper, brown sugar and cinnamon

butter

Lamb

Lamb

PAN-FRYING LAMB

Points for success

* Refer to 'Pan-frying beef' (see page 10), as techniques are the same.
* For the best flavour, oil the frying pan with a piece of fat trimmed from the chops. Spike a piece on a fork and wipe around the hot pan.
* As forequarter and neck chops tend to be fatty, after cooking skim all the fat from the pan before using the pan juices to make the gravy. Otherwise the gravy will be very fatty.
* Cook thick chops on high for 1 minute on the first side, turn and cook for 1 minute, then reduce heat to medium or low for remaining time.

STIR-FRYING LAMB

Points for success

* Refer to 'Stir-frying beef' (see page 13), as techniques are the same.
* Stir-fry in small batches (9oz/250g at a time) to prevent meat shedding its juices.
* When ready to stir-fry, add a small quantity of oil to wok or frying pan and swirl to coat base and sides. Heat until smoking.
* If a wok is not available, a heavy-based frying pan may be used. Place over small gas ring or element so heat is concentrated in one place.
* Thinly slice strips across the grain, or purchase ready-prepared stir-fry from your butcher.

ROASTING LAMB

Points for success

* Refer to 'Oven-roasting beef' (see page 11), as techniques are the same.
* Leg and shoulder roasts are always available, but if you require a rack or crown roast or boned loin or eye of loin, it is best to order it from your butcher in advance.
* It is important to skim any fat from baking dish before deglazing the dish and making gravy, otherwise the gravy may be very fatty. This is not necessary for trim lamb roasts.
* Always place the roast fat-side down in the baking dish so that when it is turned half-way through cooking to fat-side up, it will brown and crisp.
* Roast lamb at 350–375°F (180–190°C) for approximately 30 minutes per 17½oz (500g). Roast smaller trim lamb roasts at 420°F (220°C) for 10 minutes per 3½oz (100g). To test, pierce the meat with a skewer through to the centre of the thickest part. If the juices run red, the roast needs more cooking.

If the juices run clear with just a tinge of pink, a medium degree of cooking has been reached—this is ideal for lamb. If juices run clear, the lamb is well done.

* When roasting meat, it is easier to achieve the correct degree of cooking by using a meat thermometer. Place the thermometer into the thickest part of the meat, do not touch the bone. Internal temperature for lamb is 160°F (70°C) for medium and 165°F (75°C) for well done. Lamb is not at its best when rare.

Barbecuing lamb

Points for success

* Refer to 'Barbecuing beef' (see page 12), as techniques are the same.
* Cut a clove of garlic and toss it on the hot coals when barbecuing lamb—this will add a delicious subtle flavour. Likewise, a few dried herbs will produce a similar effect.Cooking time for chops and steaks will vary with the thickness of the cut and the heat of the barbecue. About 4 minutes each side is a good guide. Sear meat on the hottest part of the grill then move to a more moderate part of the barbecue. If the fire is too hot, elevate the meat.

Grilling lamb

Points for success

* Refer to 'Grilling beef' (see page 12), as techniques are the same.
* When trimming the fat off chops, leave a small border of fat around edge to help keep them moist while cooking. Slash the fat line at intervals to prevent meat curling during cooking.
* To prepare mid-loin chops, roll up the tail part to base of the T-bone, thread a skewer through the roll then diagonally across the chop. This will keep it a good shape during cooking, and make it easy to turn.
* For best results, bring meat to room temperature before grilling. Remove lamb from refrigerator 30 minutes before cooking, season immediately with pepper and herbs. Add salt after cooking.
* Marinades and glazes may be used but keep them simple, so as not to overwhelm the flavour of the lamb.
* Line your grilling tray with foil. This will prevent marinades and juices being baked onto the grill.

Lamb and Sweet Potato Stew

SERVES 4

Preheat the oven to 350°F (180°C). Trim any excess fat from the cutlets, then heat oil in a large, heavy-based frying pan and fry the cutlets for 1–2 minutes on each side until brown (you may have to do this in batches). Remove the cutlets, discard the oil and add a little stock to the pan. Bring to the boil, stirring and scraping the bottom of the pan, then add to the rest of the stock.

Place half the onions in a large ovenproof casserole dish. Top with one-third of the sweet potatoes, then add half the carrots and celery, and all the sage, thyme and cutlets. Season, then sprinkle over the barley. Repeat the layering and top with the remaining sweet potatoes. Pour over the stock and cover.

Cook for 1½ hours or until the lamb is tender, checking occasionally and adding more stock or water if the casserole is becoming too dry. Remove the lid and increase the heat to 450°F (230°C). Cook for 8–10 minutes, until the potatoes have browned.

8 lamb cutlets
1 tablespoon olive oil
2 cups chicken stock
2 onions, thinly sliced
17½oz (500g) sweet potatoes, cut into 1cm-thick slices
7oz (200g) carrots, chopped
4 sticks celery, chopped
6 fresh sage leaves
4 fresh thyme sprigs
salt and black pepper
3 tablespoons pearl barley

Roasted Leg of Lamb with Vegetables

SERVES 4

1 leg of lamb (about 1½ kg)

2 cloves garlic, cut into slivers

2 fresh rosemary sprigs, cut into
    small pieces

salt and black pepper

14oz (400g) parsnips, chopped

10½oz (300g) carrots, chopped

6 heads chicory, cut into quarters
    lengthwise

1¼ cups red or white wine

2 tablespoons red wine vinegar

Preheat the oven to 350°F (180°C). Make several incisions in the lamb using a sharp knife. Push the garlic slivers and pieces of rosemary into the incisions, then season well.

Arrange the vegetables in a large roasting tin and place the lamb on top. Pour in the wine and vinegar and roast for 2–2½ hours until the lamb is tender, basting the lamb and turning the vegetables in the cooking juices every 30 minutes. Add a little more wine or water if necessary.

Transfer the lamb to a plate, reserving the cooking juices, then cover with foil and rest for 15 minutes. Carve the lamb and serve with the vegetables, with the cooking juices drizzled over.

Baked Lamb Chops with Tomatoes

SERVES 4

Trim any excess fat from the chops. To make the marinade, place the thyme, oil, vinegar and seasoning in a non-metallic ovenproof dish. Add the chops and turn to coat. Cover and place in the refrigerator for 1 hour.

Preheat the oven to 420°F (220°C). Place the tomatoes in a bowl and cover with boiling water. Leave for 30 seconds, then peel, deseed and chop.

Mix together the tomatoes, capsicum, onion and garlic, then season well. Spoon the mixture over the chops. Bake for 35 minutes for medium-cooked chops, or 45 minutes for chops that are well done. Cover with foil and set aside for 5 minutes to rest. Garnish with fresh thyme.

4 large lamb loin chops
17½oz (500g) Roma tomatoes
1 large green bell pepper (capsicum), finely chopped
1 red onion, finely chopped
2 large cloves garlic, finely chopped
MARINADE
¼ cup fresh thyme, chopped
3 tablespoons olive oil
3 tablespoons red wine vinegar
salt and freshly ground black pepper

Lemon Pepper-crumbed Lamb Cutlets

SERVES 4

8 large lamb cutlets

1 tablespoon lemon pepper
  seasoning

2 eggs, lightly beaten

1 cup dry breadcrumbs

¼ cup canola oil

SWEET POTATO MASH

750g (1lb 10oz) sweet potato,
  peeled and chopped

30g (1oz) butter

salt and freshly ground black
  pepper

To make the sweet potato mash, place the sweet potato in a saucepan of water. Bring to the boil and simmer for 15–20 minutes or until tender. Drain and mash. Add the butter and season to taste.

Meanwhile, trim the lamb cutlets and pound with a meat mallet to flatten. Coat lightly with lemon pepper seasoning, dip in egg and coat with breadcrumbs.

Heat the oil in a large frying pan. Add the cutlets in batches and cook for 2–3 minutes on each side or until cooked to your liking. Serve the lamb cutlets with sweet potato mash and salad greens.

Moroccan Lamb Cutlets with Couscous

SERVES **3–4**

Rub cutlets with a little oil on both sides and sprinkle on both sides with the Moroccan seasoning. Place on a platter, cover and refrigerate for 20 minutes. Stand at room temperature for 15 minutes before cooking.

While lamb is standing, place the couscous in a large bowl. Bring water and salt to the boil and pour immediately over the couscous. Stir, then stand covered for 5 minutes or until all water is absorbed.

Line the steamer with a circle of baking paper larger than the base. With a skewer punch through the paper to make some holes to enable steam to enter. Spoon the couscous into the steamer. Sprinkle on the apricots, set the steamer over the skillet of boiling water and steam uncovered for 20 minutes. Add the butter and almonds and fork through.

Prepare the barbecue for two zone direct-heat cooking. Place the steamer at the side of hot plate to keep hot.

Place the cutlets on hottest part of the grill. Cook for 2 minutes. Move to second zone of grill and cook 2 minutes more. Turn cutlet with tongs, return to hotter grill and cook second side likewise.

Tip the steamer with the couscous on its side next to serving platter and pull out the paper, tipping the couscous onto the platter. Mound it high, arrange the cutlets around the couscous and serve immediately.

12 lamb cutlets, frenched
2 teaspoons olive oil
Moroccan spice mix seasoning
COUSCOUS
1½ cups instant couscous
1½ cups boiling water
½ teaspoon salt
1 tablespoon butter
5 dried apricot halves
2 tablespoons slivered almonds,
  toasted

Honey Garlic Soy Short Loin with Lime

SERVES 3–4

12 thick lamb short loin chops

¾ cup honey

1 teaspoon garlic

2 tablespoons soy sauce

SALSA

5–6 limes

2 medium-sized red onions, finely
    diced

1 cup coarsely chopped arugula
    (rocket) leaves

½ teaspoon sugar, or to taste

salt to taste

1 teaspoon chopped fresh chilli

Place the chops in a large, non-metallic dish in one layer. Cover with soy sauce, garlic and honey and marinate for 3–4 hours in refrigerator. Stand at room temperature 20 minutes before cooking.

While lamb is marinating, prepare the salsa, peel the limes, removing all pith, cut in half lengthwise. Remove core and seeds and cut into ¼in (5mm) dice.

Toss the diced lime, onions, chopped arugula, chilli and sugar together. Add salt to taste, place in a bowl and sprinkle with freshly ground black pepper. Refrigerate until serving time.

Prepare the barbecue for two-zone direct-heat cooking. Oil the grill well. Place meat on hottest part of the grill in rows and cook 4 minutes, brushing with extra marinade twice. Turn the chops, brush with extra marinade, move to second zone to complete cooking until done to your liking. Total cooking time is 6–8 minutes for medium. If marinade is charring, place a sheet of baking paper over the grill and place the chops on the baking paper.

Serve with salsa and accompany with barbecued baby sweet corn and other vegetables of choice.

Nut-crusted Lamb Racks

Trim some of the fat from the racks, leaving only a thin layer.

Place breadcrumbs into a bowl. Add butter, nuts, oregano, basil, parsley and lemon pepper. Mix to distribute ingredients evenly, then add only enough egg to just bind the mixture (not too moist). Press firmly onto each rack. Place in a tray, cover carefully with wrap, refrigerate.

Peel the sweet potato and cut diagonally into ¾in (2cm) slices. Place lamb with the onions in a foil roasting pan and drizzle with a little oil.

Prepare covered barbecue for indirect cooking. Heat coals to medium high, gas barbecue to high. Reduce heat to medium when food is placed. Place the foil tray with the sweet potato and onions on indirect heat, cover with lid or hood and cook for 15 minutes.

Open lid, move the potato tray to direct heat and turn the vegetables. Place the lamb racks in the foil tray over indirect heat or place directly onto the grill bars over a drip tray. Cover with hood and cook for 35 minutes.

Remove lamb when done and rest 10 minutes before serving. Remove vegetables. Serve the lamb racks on heated plates with a serving of vegetables.

3 lamb racks (3–4 cutlets each)
2 teaspoons oil
2 cups soft white breadcrumbs
2 tablespoons melted butter
½ cup chopped macadamia or Brazil nuts
1 teaspoon fresh oregano
1 tablespoon finely chopped fresh basil
1 tablespoon finely chopped fresh parsley
½ teaspoon lemon pepper
1 beaten egg, to bind
2 slender sweet potatoes
3 small onions, peeled and quartered with root end attached

Chump Chops with Garlic Mash

SERVES 4

6–8 lamb chump chops
RED WINE & GARLIC MARINADE
¾ cup dry red wine
½ tablespoon chopped fresh thyme
½ teaspoon salt
½ teaspoon ground black pepper
1½ tablespoons Worcestershire
  sauce
1 cloves garlic, finely chopped
½ tablespoon soy sauce
⅓ cup water
1½ teaspoons cornflour (cornstarch)
GARLIC MASH
2lb (1kg) potatoes, peeled and cut
4 teaspoons freshly crushed garlic
½ cup milk
3 tablespoons butter
salt and pepper to taste
CARMELISED ONION REDUCTION
1 tablespoons olive oil
½ onion, puréed
1 teaspoons crushed garlic
1 tablespoons butter
2 fresh bay leaves
¼ cup dry red wine
½ teaspoon balsamic vinegar
½ teaspoon honey
½ tablespoon brown sugar

To make the marinade, put all ingredients, except 2 tablespoons of water and cornflour, into a saucepan. Stir to combine and simmer for 10 minutes. Add a little of the water to the cornflour to make a paste. Add the rest of the water to the cornflour, and then add to the marinade. Stir to combine, and then simmer for a further 5 minutes. Adjust the seasoning.

To make 1 cup onion reduction, add the olive oil to a frying pan and gently fry the onion, stirring regularly for about 15–20 minutes until medium brown. Add the minced garlic and gently fry for 2–3 more minutes. Add all other ingredients and stir to combine. Season to taste. Use ½ cup.

Trim the side fat from the chops leaving a thin strip. Coat both sides with the marinade. Cover and marinate for 2 hours in the refrigerator. Bring to room temperature before cooking.

Cook the potatoes until soft in boiling salted water. Drain and mash in the skillet. Add the garlic, butter and milk.

Prepare barbecue for direct-heat cooking. Heat medium high for charcoal, high for gas, then turn to medium high.

Oil the grill bars well and place the chops on top. Cook for 6–8 minutes on each side or until done to your liking. Brush with extra marinade at intervals. Reheat the potato at side of barbecue.

To serve, place a serve of potato on each plate, lightly drizzle the surface of the potato with half of the heated red wine reduction and place on the chops on top. Pour remaining sauce down centre of chops. Serve with vegetables and garnish with finely shredded flat-leaf parsley.

Curry Yoghurt Cutlets

Preheat a barbecue to high.

Combine the yoghurt, ginger, lemon juice, garlic, curry powder and salt and pepper to taste. Marinate the lamb cutlets in the mixture for 10 minutes.

Barbecue cutlets for 3–4 minutes each side, depending on their thickness. Serve with natural yoghurt.

Chicken tenderloins can also be used in this recipe. To make a yoghurt dipping sauce, combine freshly chopped mint and a little chutney with natural yoghurt.

½ cup natural yoghurt
⅓in (1cm) piece ginger, grated
1 tablespoon lemon juice
2 cloves garlic, crushed
2 teaspoons curry powder
salt and pepper to taste
12 lean lamb cutlets
natural yoghurt to serve

Coconut Lamb Chops

SERVES 4

8 *lamb chump chops, trimmed*

14oz *(400ml) coconut milk*

2 *tablespoons crunchy peanut butter*

2 *bunches broccolini, trimmed and halved*

Preheat the oven to 400°F (200°C).

Preheat a large non-stick frying pan on high heat.

Cook the lamb chops in the frying pan for 1 minute on each side or until browned, then transfer into an ovenproof casserole dish.

Add the coconut milk and peanut butter to the pan, stir until combined and bring to the boil. Pour the coconut sauce over the lamb chops. Bake uncovered, for 35 minutes or until cooked through.

Meanwhile, place a large saucepan of water on high heat and bring to the boil. Cook the broccolini for 2 minutes or until tender.

Divide the lamb chops and broccolini evenly amongst four serving plates and serve immediately.

Lamb Racks with Smoky Aubergine Mash

SERVES 4

Preheat the grill to high.

Preheat the oven to 375°F (190°C).

Prick the eggplants with a fork, then place on a baking tray. Grill, turning occasionally, for 15 minutes until skin has blackened and insides are tender. Remove and set aside to cool. Cut the aubergines in half lengthwise. Scoop the flesh out into a medium bowl and mash with a fork. Set aside and keep warm.

Meanwhile, place the potatoes in a medium saucepan. Cover with cold water and bring to the boil. Cook for 5–10 minutes or until tender. Drain, return to the saucepan and mash. Add the aubergine and stir to combine.

Coat the lamb in dukkah and roast for 25 minutes for medium or until cooked to your liking. Transfer to a plate, cover and rest for 5 minutes. Serve with smoky aubergine mash.

NOTE

Dukkah is an Egyptian dry spice mixture of chopped nuts and seeds. It's available at specialty food stores.

4 large aubergine (eggplants)
10½oz (300g) potatoes, peeled and coarsely chopped
4 racks of lamb, French trimmed, about 9oz (250g) each
¼ cup dukkah

Lamb Chops with Cranberry and Orange SERVES 4

½ cup red wine

½ cup vegetable stock

9oz (250g) jar cranberry and
   orange sauce

½oz (15g) butter, chilled

2 teaspoons oil

12 lamb chops, trimmed of
   excess fat

SALSA

grated zest (optional) and flesh
   of 1 orange

3 scallions (spring onions), finely
   sliced

3 tablespoons chopped fresh
   parsley

1 teaspoon olive oil

Place the wine and stock in a small saucepan and bring to the boil. Boil rapidly for 5–6 minutes over a high heat or until reduced by half. Stir in the cranberry and orange sauce and boil for a further 2–3 minutes, until thick. Remove the pan from the heat and stir in the chilled butter. Set aside.

To prepare the salsa, peel the orange using a small sharp knife, then cut away the flesh into segments. Chop these into small pieces and combine with the remaining ingredients in a bowl.

Heat the oil in a large, non-stick frying pan over a high heat, add half the lamb chops and cook for 3–4 minutes on one side, until browned. Remove from pan and repeat with remaining chops. Return all the chops to the pan. Pour in half the sauce and simmer for 2 minutes, until cooked through and hot. Serve browned-side up with the salsa and extra sauce poured over the chops, accompanied by fresh green beans.

NOTE

Many people prefer the flavour of organic lamb. Like all red meats, it is an excellent source of iron, zinc and protein. Lamb is slightly fattier than pork or beef, so you may want to trim off some of the fat. The succulent lamb chops are cooked with a cranberry and orange sauce. Serving them with the lively orange salsa adds a really bright and refreshing touch.

Barbecued Port-glazed Lamb

SERVES 8

Preheat covered barbecue to a medium heat.

Place lamb on a wire rack set in a roasting tin and brush with glaze. Pour port wine and water into roasting tin, cover barbecue with lid and cook for 2 hours, brushing with glaze at 15 minute intervals, or until cooked to your liking.

To make the port glaze, place mustard, orange rind, nutmeg, port wine, honey and vinegar in a saucepan, bring to simmering over a low heat and simmer until mixture thickens and reduces slightly.

5lb 8oz (2½kg) leg of lamb
9fl oz (250ml) port
13fl oz (375ml) water
PORT GLAZE
4 tablespoons Dijon mustard
2 teaspoons finely grated orange rind
½ teaspoon grated nutmeg
13fl oz (375ml) port wine
4fl oz (125ml) honey
2 tablespoons balsamic vinegar

Lamb Shanks with Root Vegetables

SERVES 4

2 tablespoons olive oil

2 parsnips, peeled and cut into
   large chunks

1 medium sweet potato, peeled
   and cut into large chunks

1 swede, peeled and cut into large
   chunks

1 bunch scallions (spring onions),
   trimmed

2 cloves garlic, crushed

4 lamb shanks

¾ cup beef stock

¼ cup water

½ cup red wine

1 tablespoon tomato paste

2 sprigs rosemary, leaves removed
   and chopped

1 bouquet garni

freshly ground pepper and salt

Heat 1 tablespoon oil in a large heavy-based saucepan, add root vegetables and scallions and cook quickly until brown. Set aside on a plate. Add the remaining oil to the pan and brown the garlic and shanks for a few minutes.

Add the stock, water, wine, tomato paste, rosemary, bouquet garni, pepper and salt. Bring to the boil, reduce the heat, and leave to simmer with the lid on for 20 minutes.

Return vegetables to the pan and continue to cook for another 30 minutes, until vegetables and lamb are cooked.

Before serving, remove the bouquet garni and season to taste.

Lamb Osso Bucco

Preheat the oven to 320°F (160°C). Mix together the flour, salt and pepper on a plate. Dip the lamb pieces into the mixture to coat well. Heat 1 tablespoon of the oil in a large heavy-based frying pan until hot but not smoking. Add the lamb and cook over a medium-high heat for 5–8 minutes, turning frequently until browned on all sides. Transfer to a deep ovenproof dish.

Heat the remaining oil in the pan, add the onion, carrot and celery and cook over a low heat for 4–5 minutes, until softened. Add the tomatoes, tomato purée, wine and stock and bring to the boil, stirring occasionally. Pour over the lamb, cover with foil and bake for 1–2 hours until the meat is tender, turning it over halfway through. Season to taste.

To make the gremolata, mix together the parsley, mint, lemon zest and garlic. Sprinkle over the lamb and serve.

2 tablespoons all-purpose (plain) flour
salt and black pepper
4 lamb shanks, trimmed of excess fat
2 tablespoons olive oil
1 onion, finely chopped
1 carrot, finely chopped
1 stick celery, finely chopped
14oz (400g) canned chopped tomatoes with herbs
1 tablespoon sun-dried tomato purée
½ cup dry white wine
2 cups lamb stock
GREMOLATA
¼ cup fresh parsley, chopped
¼ cup fresh mint, chopped
finely grated zest of 1 lemon
1 clove garlic, finely chopped

Lamb Cutlets with Olives and Rosemary

SERVES 4

1 tablespoon olive oil

2 cloves garlic, minced

8–12 lamb cutlets, depending on size

⅔ cup dry white wine

2 tablespoons tomato paste

⅔ cup beef stock

2 sprigs rosemary, roughly chopped

⅓ cup black olives

freshly ground black pepper

Preheat oven to 350°F (180°C).

Heat the oil in a large pan, add garlic and lamb cutlets, and brown, on medium heat for 2–3 minutes on each side.

Add wine and cook for 2 minutes. Mix the tomato paste with the beef stock and add to the lamb cutlets. Add the rosemary, black olives and pepper.

Transfer lamb to a casserole dish and bake for 30–40 minutes.

Braised Shoulder of Lamb

Preheat oven to 340°F (170°C).

Mix together 2 tablespoons olive oil, garlic and rosemary. Brush mixture over lamb. If meat is too big for your casserole dish, roll up and secure with string.

Heat remaining oil in a large heavy-based flame-proof casserole dish over medium to high heat. Add meat and brown quickly on both sides. Add port and reduce by half.

Add stock, tomatoes, carrots, celery and onions. Bring to the boil. Remove from heat. Cover with foil or a lid and bake in the oven for 2 hours or until lamb is tender.

Cut meat into slices and serve with vegetables and bread.

2fl oz (60ml) olive oil

2 cloves garlic, crushed

2 teaspoons freshly chopped rosemary

3lb 5oz (1.5kg) lamb shoulder, deboned

4fl oz (125ml) port wine

4fl oz (125ml) beef stock

14oz (400g) can diced tomatoes

2 carrots, peeled and chopped

3 celery stalks, chopped

8 scallions (spring onions), trimmed

salt and freshly ground black pepper

Braised Lamb Shanks with Roasted Tomatoes

SERVES 4

4 lamb shanks

1 cup Arborio rice

2 carrots

2 stalks celery, sliced

8 tomatoes

1 teaspoon minced chilli

2 cups beef stock

1 cup red wine

2 teaspoons dried rosemary

4 small garlic bulbs

1 tablespoon oil

¼ cup parsley, chopped

Preheat oven to 400°F (200°C). Place lamb shanks in a roasting dish. Bake for 30 minutes. Place rice in the bottom of a large casserole dish.

Sprinkle carrots and celery over rice. Cut tomato skin around middle. Mix chilli, stock, wine and rosemary together. Pour over rice. Drain fat from shanks and place shanks on top of rice with tomatoes. Cover and cook at 300°F (150°C) for 2 hours.

Wash and dry garlic bulbs. Brush garlic with oil. Place in an ovenproof dish and pour in a quarter of a cup of water.

Cover and cook alongside shanks for 1 hour or until soft. Serve shanks with a bulb of garlic for each person. Garnish with chopped parsley.

NOTE

To eat the garlic, squeeze the soft flesh out of the skin.

Burgundy Lamb Shanks

SERVES 4

Season shanks with salt, pepper, lemon zest and oregano. Place in the slow cooker and sprinkle with garlic and parsley.

In a heavy-based frying pan, sauté carrot and onion in oil and transfer to slow cooker. Pour wine into frying pan and add stock cube. Deglaze frying pan and stir juices into slow cooker.

Cover and cook on low for 8 hours. If you wish to have a thicker sauce, drain cooking liquid into a saucepan and boil to reduce and thicken slightly.

4lb 6oz (2kg) lamb shanks
salt and freshly ground black
* pepper*
grated zest of ½ lemon
½ teaspoon dried oregano
2 cloves garlic, minced
¼ cup fresh parsley, chopped
1 carrot, peeled and chopped
1 onion, chopped
1 teaspoon olive oil
1 cup dry red wine
1 beef stock cube, crumbled

Lamb Racks with Spicy Asian Plum Sauce

SERVES 4-5

2 scallions (spring onions)

4 lamb racks each with 4 chops

1 teaspoon sesame oil

SPICY ASIAN PLUM SAUCE

½ cup plum jam

2 tablespoons soy sauce

1 tablespoon grated root ginger

2 tablespoons white vinegar

½ teaspoon Chinese five-spice
   powder

¼ cup beef stock

To make the plum sauce, place jam, soy sauce, ginger, vinegar, five-spice powder and beef stock in a saucepan. Mix to combine. Bring to the boil and simmer for 10 minutes or until syrupy.

Trim scallions. Cut into thin lengths and place in iced water while preparing rest of meal. Trim silverskin from lamb. Brush lamb with sesame oil. Bake at 430°F (220°C) for 15–20 minutes. Stand for 5 minutes. Serve on sweet potato mash with Spicy Asian Plum Sauce spooned over and garnished with drained scallions.

Lamb Shanks with Carrots and Parsnips

Preheat the oven to 340°F (170°C).

Heat half the oil in a large frying pan to medium-high. Add onions, carrots and parsnips and brown quickly. Remove the vegetables and set aside.

Coat the lamb shanks in Tuscan seasoning. Heat the remaining oil and brown the lamb shanks.

Transfer the lamb shanks to a large heavy-based baking dish. Pour in the beef stock, wine and bay leaves. Cover with foil and bake in the oven for 2 hours, adding more stock or water as needed. Add the vegetables in the last 25–30 minutes. Bake until the lamb and vegetables are tender.

Serve the shanks with pan juices, vegetables and potato mash.

NOTE

You can use other root vegetables such as turnips and swedes. These are in season from May to August. Lamb shanks are best cooked very slowly until tender and the meat starts to fall off the bone.

2fl oz (60ml) olive oil

1 onion, cut into 8 wedges

2 medium carrots, peeled and cut into quarters

2 medium parsnips, peeled and cut into quarters

4 lamb shanks

1 tablespoon Tuscan seasoning

17½fl oz (500ml) beef stock

4fl oz (125ml) red wine

4 bay leaves

Lamb Shanks with Plum and Thyme

SERVES 4

4 lamb shanks
fresh thyme for garnish
PLUM AND THYME SAUCE
1 small onion
½ cup plum jam
2 tablespoons balsamic vinegar
¼ cup beef stock
1 teaspoon fresh or dried thyme
  leaves
freshly ground black pepper

To make the plum and thyme sauce, peel onion and chop finely. Dry fry in a Teflon-coated frying pan. Add plum jam, vinegar, beef stock and thyme to pan. Grind black pepper over. Simmer for 5 minutes or until slightly thickened. Serve hot.

Place lamb shanks on a rack over a roasting dish. A grill rack is good for this. Slow roast at 300°F (150°C) for 40 minutes. Remove from oven. When cool enough to handle cut any remaining fat from shanks leaving meat only on bone. Return to oven and bake at 350°F (180°C) for a further 50 minutes or until cooked. Serve on a sweet potato mash with Plum and Thyme Sauce spooned over. Garnish with fresh thyme.

NOTE
Lamb shanks are a favourite food for many. Don't think you have to leave them out of a diet that looks after your weight. Try this cooking style for a lamb shank treat.

Lamb Shanks with Red Wine

Trim excess fat from the lamb shanks.

Place the onions and garlic in a slow cooker bowl. Put flour in a plastic bag with the lamb shanks, shake to completely coat the shanks and then place shanks in the cooker on top of the onions and garlic. Sprinkle any leftover flour over the top.

Combine all other ingredients in a small bowl and mix thoroughly, then spoon this over the shanks in the cooker.

Place lid on and cook on high for 4–5 hours or on low for 9–10 hours. Serve with green beans and mashed potatoes.

6 lamb shanks
2 medium onions, chopped
2 cloves garlic, crushed
¼ cup plain (all-purpose) flour
¼ cup fresh coriander (cilantro), chopped
¼ cup beef stock
¾ cup red wine
2 tablespoons tomato paste
juice and zest of 1 orange
3 large sprigs fresh rosemary, leaves removed and chopped

Slow-Simmered Lamb Shanks with Lentils

SERVES 4

4 lamb shanks

2 large onions, diced

¾ cup beef stock

½ cup dry white wine

14oz (400g) canned chopped
  tomatoes

2 bay leaves

4 sprigs fresh thyme

1 cinnamon stick

7oz (200g) pumpkin, diced

2 courgettes (zucchini), diced

6 dried apricots, diced

1½ cups lentils

Heat a large frying pan over high heat and add the lamb shanks in batches, cook until browned. Transfer to a slow cooker set on high. Add the onions to the frying pan, reduce the heat to medium and cook for 3 minutes.

Add the beef stock to the frying pan to collect up all the pan flavours, then add stock and onion to the slow cooker.

Add the wine, tomatoes, bay leaves, thyme and cinnamon stick to slow cooker. Cover and cook for 3 hours.

Add the pumpkin, courgette, apricots and lentils and cook for a further 2 hours on a low setting or until the vegetables are tender and the lamb starts to come away from the bone. Serve with crusty bread.

Indonesian Barbecued Lamb Cutlets

Combine oil, lemon juice, soy sauce, garlic, coriander and cumin to make marinade. Place lamb cutlets in a dish. Pour marinade over and marinate in the refrigerator for 2–3 hours.

Cook lamb cutlets on a barbecue plate for 8–10 minutes, occasionally basting.

Serve with fried rice (nasi goreng) and quick peanut sauce (saus kacang cepat).

2 tablespoons peanut oil
¼ cup lemon juice
1 tablespoon soy sauce
2 cloves garlic, crushed
1 teaspoon ground coriander
1 teaspoon ground cumin
8 lamb cutlets

Lemon Pepper Lamb Cutlets

SERVES 2–3

6–9 lamb cutlets
2 teaspoons lemon pepper
   seasoning
1 teaspoon olive oil
lemon juice for serving

Trim any fat off the cutlets and pound a little with a meat mallet to even out.

Mix the lemon pepper with the oil. Using your fingers, rub the mixture into both sides of the cutlets and sprinkle a little extra lemon pepper on top.

Cut a circle of baking paper a little larger than the base of a large frying pan. Heat the frying pan then fit in the paper. Place the cutlets in the pan immediately and cook on medium heat for 3–5 minutes on each side or until done to your liking.

Remove to a heated plate, sprinkle with lemon juice. Serve immediately with vegetable accompaniments.

Herb and Garlic Lamb Shanks

SERVES 4

Score the outside of the lamb shanks and rub crushed garlic and Dijon mustard into them. In a heavy-based frying pan, heat the olive oil and brown the lamb shanks.

Place the browned lamb in the slow cooker, then pour in the chicken stock and sprinkle the herbs over the lamb. Add salt and freshly ground black pepper to taste, Cook on low for 8–9 hours or 4–5 hours on high.

4 meaty lamb shanks
2 cloves garlic, crushed
1 tablespoon Dijon mustard
2 tablespoons olive oil
3 cups chicken stock
2 teaspoons dried rosemary
2 teaspoons dried Italian herbs
salt and freshly ground black
*   pepper*

Irish Stew

3 carrots, thinly sliced

2 onions, thinly sliced

17½oz (500g) potatoes, thinly
   sliced

8 lamb neck chops

salt and freshly ground black
   pepper

2 bay leaves

2 cups chicken stock simmering

Put all the vegetables into the slow cooker. Trim the chops of any excess fat and lay these on top of the vegetables. Add the seasoning, bay leaves and stock.

Cover and cook for 6–8 hours on high or 10–14 hours on low.

Lamb Boulangère

SERVES 4-5

Layer vegetables in slow cooker, seasoning and adding thyme sprigs between layers.

Rub cut surfaces of garlic well over lamb, then season and place on vegetable bed. Pour in stock and cook on low for approximately 8–10 hours. Skim as much fat as possible from surface of liquid and serve lamb in thick slices, with vegetables and juices spooned over.

NOTE
If preferred, lamb may be browned in a hot oven just before serving.

2 white onions, thinly sliced
2 potatoes, thinly sliced
2 tomatoes, peeled and sliced
salt and freshly ground black
  pepper
½ bunch thyme
1 clove garlic, quartered
1 small leg of lamb, trimmed of
  fat and gristle
4oz (125fl oz) cup beef stock

Greek Lamb Platter

8 lamb cutlets, trimmed
lemon pepper seasoning
ground oregano leaves
3 cup tzatziki, to serve
Greek salad, to serve
country-style bread, sliced ⅓in
*   (1cm) thick and toasted on*
*   barbecue*
SOUVLAKI
1 lamb leg tip approximately 1lb
*   16oz (900g) cut into ¾in (2cm)*
*   cubes*
½ cup store-bought red wine and
*   garlic marinade, mixed with*
*   ½ cup lemon juice*
1 bay leaf
KEFTE
2lb 4oz (1kg) minced lamb
¼ cup dried breadcrumbs
1 teaspoon greek seasoning
¼ teaspoon cinnamon
1 teaspoon onion flakes

To prepare the cutlets, flatten out if needed. Rub over with a little oil, sprinkle both sides with lemon pepper and oregano. Place single layer on a tray. Cover and refrigerate until ready to use.

To prepare the souvlaki, cut the lamb tip into ¾in (2cm) cubes. Place in a bowl, pour over the marinade-lemon juice mixture. Add bay leaf, cover and marinate in refrigerator for several hours, stir occasionally.

To prepare the kefte, combine all ingredients, knead well with hand for several minutes to make a fine grain mixture. With damp hands roll into oval shapes about 2¹/₃in (6cm) long. Place on a tray, cover and refrigerate.

Prepare the barbecue for direct heat cooking on to high. Oil the grill bars and grill plate well. Place the 3 meats on the grill in an orderly fashion and cook for the times given below. Two people will be needed to turn the foods.

Cutlets: 3 to 4 minutes each side

Souvlaki: 6 minutes each side

Kefte: 5 to 6 minutes each side

To serve, prepare a large platter or tray. Place the tzatziki in bowls in centre, salad at one end of platter and arrange the 3 meats at other end. Serve hot bread in a bread basket.

Lamb Cutlets with Garlic Mash

SERVES 3-4

Place lamb cutlets on a platter. Whisk the lemon juice, oil, oregano Leaves and salt together. Brush onto both sides of the cutlets. Grind pepper onto both sides. Stand at room temperature for 30 minutes.

Meanwhile, prepare the mash. Place the potatoes on to boil. Heat oil in a small pan, add onions and stir to coat well with oil. Reduce heat to low, cover with a lid and cook 6 minutes to sweat the onions to soften. Remove lid, increase heat, add garlic, stir continuously until onions are a rich golden colour.

When potatoes are tender, drain and mash with the milk and butter. Stir in the onion garlic mixture and Parmesan cheese. Keep hot.

Heat the barbecue grill to hot, spray surface with oil spray. Place on the cutlets and cook for 2 to 3 minutes each side or to your liking, brushing frequently with any remaining oil lemon mixture.

Heat the finishing sauce according to packet instructions.

To serve, place a mound of garlic mash on each plate. Place 3 to 4 cutlets on top and drizzle over with the finishing sauce. Garnish with arugula leaves.

12 lamb cutlets or loin chops
1 tablespoon lemon juice
1 tablespoon oil
salt to taste
1 teaspoon dried oregano
dash of black pepper
GARLIC MASH
1 teaspoon oil
1 large onion, finely diced
2 teaspoons freshly crushed garlic
1lb 10oz (750g) potatoes, peeled and cut into even sizes
½ cup milk
1 tablespoon butter
2 tablespoons grated Parmesan cheese
caramelised onion reduction (see Chump Chops with Garlic Mash)
small bunch of arugula (rocket), to serve

Lamb Chops with Prunes

SERVES 4

1 medium onion, finely chopped

1 teaspoon olive oil

4 large lamb chops

salt and freshly ground black
    pepper

¾in (2cm) piece fresh ginger,
    minced

½ teaspoon ground cumin

2 cloves garlic, minced

1 whole cinnamon stick

¼ cup fresh cilantro (coriander),
    chopped

1 cup pitted prunes

2 tablespoons honey

1½ tablespoons lime juice

2 tablespoons toasted sesame
    seeds

In a large heavy-based frying pan, sauté onion in oil until limp. Brown lamb chops well on both sides. Season with salt and pepper. Add ginger, cumin, garlic and cinnamon stick. Sauté for 1 minute.

Transfer to the slow cooker. Add 2 tablespoons water to frying pan and deglaze. Add to slow cooker. Scatter cilantro and prunes over lamb chops. Cover and cook on low for 6 hours.

Stir in honey and lime juice. Heat to serving temperature, sprinkle with sesame seeds and serve.

Poultry

Poultry

STORAGE

REFRIGERATION	Correct storage of chicken, uncooked or cooked, is vital to avoid spoilage and waste. Fresh chicken from your butcher can be stored in the refrigerator for up to 4 days.
FREEZING	If freezing, use ziplock bags with all the air squeezed out. Frozen chicken can be stored for up to 3 months.
THAWING	When required, move chicken from freezer to refrigerator and allow to thaw evenly overnight. For faster thawing, you can defrost by putting poultry in an airtight bag and placing in a bowl or sink full of cold water, changing the water every half-hour (never use hot water).
COOKED CHICKEN	Cooked chicken should be covered or wrapped in cling wrap and placed in the refrigerator within thirty minutes of cooking. It will keep perfectly for several days. It can also be wrapped, airtight, frozen and stored for up to one month.

PAN-FRYING CHICKEN

Points for success

* Heat oil and pan well. Since they are thicker, cook breasts longer and use a lower heat than for thighs or tenderloins.
* Always deglaze the pan (dissolve the meat juices that have stuck to the base of the pan) with stock, water, wine, lemon or fruit juices. This makes a quick and easy sauce. Butter, sour cream or yoghurt can then be added to make a richer sauce

STIR-FRYING CHICKEN

Points for success

* Stir-fry in small batches (7–10½oz/200–300g) to prevent the chicken shedding its juices.
* When ready to stir-fry, add a small quantity of oil to wok or frying pan and swirl to coat base and sides.

* Heat until smoking. If a wok is not available, a heavy-based frying pan may be used. Place over the small gas ring or element so that the heat is concentrated in the centre of the pan.

ROASTING CHICKEN

Points for success

* Whole chickens are sometimes sold with the giblets and neck inside the cavity. Be sure to remove these.
* Always truss your chicken to ensure even cooking. To do this, take the wing tips and fold them back over themselves, so they tuck behind the bird. Tie the ends of the legs together firmly with a piece of string.
* Even if trussed correctly, chickens can still dry out in the oven. To avoid this you can either layer strips of bacon over the surface of the chicken, baste often with pan juices, or use an oven bag. Stuffing your chicken will also help retain moisture.
* The chicken is cooked when thickest part of the flesh is pierced with a skewer and the juices run clear.

BARBECUING CHICKEN

Points for success

* Lightly oil grill or plate to prevent chicken sticking.
* Marinate chicken if desired, to add flavour. Baste with more marinade during cooking.
* If cooking chicken with the skin on, be aware that it will drip fat. If cooking over flame, this can lead to flare-ups.

GRILLING CHICKEN

Points for success

* Season chicken with pepper and herbs before cooking, sprinkle with salt after cooking. For extra flavour, the chicken may be rubbed with a little crushed garlic.
* To keep chicken moist, brush with a little olive oil just before grilling.
* Heat grill to very hot for approximately 5 minutes before placing the chicken under. Do not leave the grill pan under the heat while heating the grill. The pan should be cold when the chicken is placed on it so the meat will not stick.
* Leave grill door open while grilling
* If grilling chicken with the skin on, be aware that fat in the skin will heat up very quickly and can cause it to char. Make sure the chicken is far enough away from the flame to avoid this.

Quick Sesame Chicken Wings

MAKES 24

Combine honey, soy sauce, sherry, ginger and garlic together. Stir together to make marinade.

Place wings in a large container. Cover with marinade for 1 hour in the refrigerator.

Place half the wings in a microwave-safe dish and microwave for 7 minutes on high. Remove and microwave the remainder.

Heat the barbecue until hot. Place a wire cake-rack over the grill bars and place the wings on the rack. Brush with marinade left in the bow. Turn and brush the wings frequently for 6 minutes until brown and crisp. While wings are crisping, spread sesame seeds on a foil tray and place on the barbecue. Shake occasionally as they toast. Sprinkle over the chicken wings and serve.

4lb (2kg) chicken wings, tips
* removed*
½ cup honey
3 tablespoons light soy sauce
2 tablespoons sherry
½ teaspoon fresh ginger, minced
½ teapoon fresh garlic, minced
3 tablespoons sesame seeds,
* toasted*

Barbecued Drumsticks with Asian Sauce

SERVES 6–8

4lb (2kg) chicken drumsticks,
    medium size

½ cup fresh lemon juice

1 tablespoon salad oil

1 teaspoon herb salt

½ cup honey

3 tablespoons soy sauce

1 teaspoon freshly chopped garlic

1 teaspoon freshly chopped ginger

4oz (125g) fresh baby corn

4 scallions (spring onions) (not
    too thin), trimmed and sliced
    on sharp diagonal

Place drumstick in a large non-metallic container, preferably in one layer. Mix lemon juice, oil, ginger, garlic, herb salt, honey and soy together. Pour over the drumsticks, reserving a small quantity to coat the vegetables. Coat both sides of the drumstick, cover and marinate in the refrigerator for several hours or overnight. Turn in the marinade at least once if you have a double layer, move the top layer to the bottom. Stand at room temperature 20 minutes before cooking.

Prepare scallions, and baby corn. Take chicken and vegetables to barbecue area.

Prepare barbecue for indirect-heat cooking. Place a drip pan containing 1 cup of water in place. Place the drumsticks directly onto the well-oiled grill bars over the drip pan. Cook for 30 minutes with lid on, and then for 30 minutes with lid off. Brush drumsticks with the extra marinade and turn.

Close lid, cook 8–10 minutes, turn and brush with marinade and repeat every 10 minutes for a total of 40 minutes or until cooked through to the bone.

In the last 10 minutes of cooking, place a sheet of foil on grill bars over direct heat. Place on the baby corn. Brush with marinade and cook 5 minutes. Turn, brush with marinade. Place on the scallion slices, splash with a little marinade and toss. Serve hot.

Tasty Chicken Wings

Place wings in a large stainless steel baking dish. Combine honey, orange juice, herbs, soy sauce and allspice to form marinade and pour over the wings. Coat both sides. Cover and marinate in refrigerator for at least 4 hours or, preferably, overnight. Prepare limes and scallions and take with chicken to the barbecue area.

Prepare barbecue for indirect-heat cooking and heat to medium. Add half cup of water to the wings in the dish. Turn and mix through, then spread wings to a single layer. Cover with a lid, and place over indirect heat for 45–50 minutes. Turn wings occasionally.

Lift the wings with tongs and place on well-oiled grill bars over direct heat for 1–2 minutes each side to crisp.

Place lime slices on grill for 1 minute each side, brushing with a little marinade. Remove chicken wings to a platter, garnish with lime slices and sprinkle with scallions.

4lb (2kg) chicken wings
1¼ cups honey
juice of 1 orange
1 tablespoon finely chopped fresh parsley
1 tablespoon finely chopped fresh oregano
1 teaspoon allspice
2 teaspoons soy sauce
2 limes, sliced into thin circles
2 scallions (spring onions), diagonally sliced

Cajun Chicken

SERVES 4

4 chicken breasts on the bone,
*   skin in*
1 tablespoon olive oil
2 tablespoons Cajun spice
1 tablespoon barbecue sauce
2 aubergine (eggplant), cut into
*   ¾in- (1.5cm) thick round slices*
½ cup store-bought tomato and
*   chilli pickle*
2 sprigs fresh oregano

Rinse the chicken, pat well to dry If necessary, smooth the skin over the breast.

Rub the chicken all over with oil, then rub the Cajun spices over with fingers, massaging in. Place in deep container, skin side up. Cover with lid or wrap that does not touch the top of the chicken. Refrigerate for 2 hours or more or just stand at room temperature for 20 minutes, then cook. Longer marinating time increases flavor.

Cut aubergine slices just before cooking. Have oil and brush ready. Take all to the barbecue area, including barbecue sauce and pickle.

Prepare barbecue for indirect-heat cooking; Insert a drip tray. Heat to medium.

Place the chicken breasts, skin side up, onto the oiled grill over the drip tray. Close the lid or hood and cook for 40 minutes; no need to turn. During the final cooking, open lid and brush lightly with barbecue sauce a few times to give a glaze. Chicken is cooked when juices run clear when pricked with a skewer. Remove from grill and keep hot.

Before the final cooking, place a shallow oven tray over the direct heat section. When it is hot, brush with oil. Brush the aubergine on both sides with oil and place on the hot tray, turn and cook other side after 2 minutes. Remove when done. Serve the chicken on a bed of aubergine. Place a tablespoon of pickle on top of each chicken breast and garnish with a sprig of fresh oregano.

Tandoori Chicken Pieces

SERVES 4

Prick the meat all over with a skewer. Sprinkle lightly with salt.

Mix the yogurt with 4 tablespoons of the tandoori paste, adding more to taste if desired. With fingers, rub mixture all over the chicken pieces, rubbing well into the slashes. Place into a non-metallic dish, cover and marinate in refrigerator for 6 hours or overnight.

Place chicken on a greased baking tray. Pour the excess marinade from the dish into a bowl. Stir butter or ghee into the marinade. Transfer all to the barbecue area.

Prepare the barbecue for indirect-heat cooking. Set up a drip pan with a cup of water in the pan.

Place the chicken on the well-oiled grill bars over the drip pan. Cover and cook for 40 minutes or until cooked. Brush with the reserved marinade at 10 minute intervals for first half of cooking, then at 5 minute intervals. At the last 5 minutes, place flatbreads into barbecue to heat over direct heat.

Remove from grill. Place on a platter lined with lettuce leaves. Garnish with lemon slices. Cut each flatbread into 6 triangular pieces and serve with the tandoori chicken.

6 chicken Maryland pieces, skin off
salt
7fl oz (200ml) natural yoghurt
tandoori paste, to taste
1 tablespoon butter or ghee, melted
crisp lettuce leaves
1 lemon
1 packet flatbread (Lebanese bread)

Teriyaki Chicken Drummettes

20 chicken drummettes
½ cup teriyaki sauce
2 courgette (zucchini)
2 heads broccoli
2 bunches bok choy

Place the chicken drummettes in a shallow dish. Pour over the marinade, then place in the refrigerator for 3 hours.

Prepare the vegetables. Wash and slice the courgette on the diagonal ¾in (1.5cm) thick, wash, then cut the broccoli into small pieces. Remove the large outer leaves of the bokchoy and wash under running water. Do not shake off the excess water, which will help the cooking process.

Prepare the barbecue for direct-heat cooking. Oil the grill well. Place on the marinated drummettes. Cook, turning regularly, for 10–12 minutes. At the same time, place on the vegetables and brush with extra marinade. Remove once the vegetables are crisp and tender. Serve on a dinner plate, placing the chicken drummettes in a pile on top of the vegetables.

Honey Mustard Chicken Drumettes

MAKES **12**

Combine the honey, tamari and mustard in a large microwave container. Heat for 30–50 seconds and stir to combine.

Toss the chicken drumettes in the honey mixture, making sure each one is well coated. Cover and cook for 10–12 minutes, stirring after 5 minutes. Garnish with scallions.

Serve on a bed of shredded red and green cabbage. Plenty of serviettes please!

½ cup honey

¼ cup tamari

1 tablespoon German mustard

17½oz (500g) chicken drumettes

scallions (spring onions), finely
  chopped, to garnish

Roast Lemon Chicken with Couscous

SERVES 4

1 whole chicken, about 4lb 6oz
  (2kg)
3 lemons
1¾ cups chicken stock
1½ cups couscous

Preheat the oven 375°F (190°C).

Remove any excess fat from the chicken cavity. Tie the chicken legs together using unwaxed kitchen string and place in a large roasting tray.

Juice two of the lemons into a small bowl and add ¼ cup of the chicken stock. Pour over the chicken. Cut the remaining lemon in half and place one half in the chicken cavity. Slice the remaining half and arrange over the chicken. Roast, basting occasionally, for 1½ hours or until juices run clear from the thigh when pricked with a skewer.

Meanwhile, pour the chicken stock into a small saucepan and bring to the boil. Add the couscous, remove from the heat and cover with cling wrap. Leave to stand for 5 minutes or until liquid is completely absorbed. Stir gently with a fork to separate the grains.

Serve the roast chicken with couscous.

Garlic Chicken

Preheat the oven to 350°F (180°C).

Place the butter, garlic and parsley in a small bowl and stir to combine.

Put the garlic butter under the chicken skin. Place the chicken breasts skin-side up and bake for 20–25 minutes until cooked through.

3oz (90g) butter, softened

6 cloves garlic, crushed

½ cup fresh parsley leaves, finely chopped

4 chicken breasts on the bone, skin on

Honey Mustard Chicken with Roast Potatoes

SERVES 4

4 chicken leg quarters
¾ cup honey mustard marinade
17½oz (500g) new potatoes
3 tablespoons olive oil

Place the chicken in a medium bowl and coat with marinade. Cover with cling wrap and refrigerate for 2 hours or until required.

Preheat the oven to 400°F (200°C).

Place the potatoes in a large saucepan and cover with water. Bring to the boil and cook for 5 minutes. Drain and place in a roasting dish. Pour in the olive oil and toss to coat. Roast for 30 minutes or until golden brown.

Meanwhile, preheat a large non-stick frying pan on medium-high heat. Cook the chicken legs for 2 minutes on each side or until browned. Transfer to an ovenproof dish and bake for 20 minutes or until cooked through. Serve the chicken with the roast potatoes.

Apricot and Citrus Glazed Chicken

SERVES 4

Place the chicken in a flameproof casserole dish, cover with the stock and bring to the boil. Lower the heat, cover and simmer for 35 minutes or until the chicken is cooked through.

Warm the jam in a saucepan for 1–2 minutes, then press through a sieve into a clean pan. Add the butter, orange and lime or lemon zest and heat for 1–2 minutes, until the butter has melted. Remove from the heat and stir in the soy sauce.

Preheat the grill to high. Remove the chicken from the poaching liquid and pat dry with absorbent paper. Remove the gristle from the end of each drumstick. Place the chicken in the base of a grill pan. Pour over the glaze and grill for 3–5 minutes, until golden brown and crisp. Serve it with rice and shredded savoy cabbage.

NOTE
Citrus fruits and a glaze of apricot jam give this gently poached chicken a sweet tangy flavour and a lovely crispy skin.

4 chicken leg joints, about 9oz (250g) each
5 cups chicken stock
2 tablespoons apricot jam
1oz (30g) butter
finely grated zest of 1 orange
finely grated zest of 1 lime or lemon
1–2 teaspoons light soy sauce

Duck with Braised Turnips

SERVES 4

4 duck leg joints

17½oz (500g) white turnips,
  peeled and cut into 2in (5cm)
  chunks

salt and freshly ground black
  pepper

½ cup chicken stock

1 teaspoon caster sugar

1 tablespoon fresh orange juice

Preheat the oven to 375°F (190°C). Heat a non-stick frying pan, add the duck, skin-side down, then cook over a medium-high heat for 7–8 minutes, until browned. Pour off the fat and reserve it. Place the duck, skin-side up, on a baking sheet and bake for 30–40 minutes, until the skin is crisp and the meat cooked through.

Meanwhile, cook the turnips in boiling salted water for 5–6 minutes, until softened, then drain. Place 2 tablespoons of the reserved duck fat in a large frying pan, add the turnips and fry for 5 minutes or until lightly browned. Add the stock and season.

Partly cover the pan and cook for 10 minutes or until the turnips are tender and almost all the liquid has evaporated. Uncover the pan, add the sugar and orange juice, then cook over a high heat for 3–4 minutes, stirring, until the turnips caramelise. Serve with the duck.

Grilled Chicken with Orange

Melt the butter in a small pan. Rub the chicken with the cut lemon, brush it liberally with melted butter and sprinkle lightly with salt.

Preheat the grill to medium. Place the chicken, inner side up, in the grill pan (with the rack removed) about 4in (10cm) below the heat. Cook for 10–12 minutes then turn it skin side up and cook for a further 10–15 minutes, brushing with butter several times during cooking. The chicken is ready when the skin is crisp and golden and the juices run colourless when the thickest part of the flesh is pierced with a skewer. Young chickens have a lot of blood in their legs, which makes their flesh pinkish; don't be misled by this into overcooking them.

To make the dressing, squeeze the juice from the half lemon into the rest of the butter—add a little more butter if necessary. Pile the pea shoots on a platter or individual plates. Serve the chicken on top with the dressing poured over. Garnish with the orange slices.

NOTE
Snow pea shoots are available at many greengrocers. Watercress or shredded lettuce is an alternative.

2oz (55g) butter
6 chicken joints, breasts, thighs or Marylands (thigh and drumsticks)
½ lemon
salt
1 packet of snow pea shoots
1 large orange, thinly sliced

Roasted Spatchcock with Rosemary

SERVES 4

*2 x no. 5 spatchcocks (each
   17½oz/500g, halved)*
MARINADE
¼ cup extra virgin olive oil
2 tablespoons lemon juice
*1 tablespoon rosemary, roughly
   chopped*
1 clove garlic, crushed
black pepper, freshly ground

Combine the marinade ingredients.

Place the spatchcocks in a large dish, pour the marinade over them, and leave to chill in the refrigerator for 3–4 hours.

Preheat the oven to 350°F (180°C).

Place the spatchcocks on a roasting rack over a roasting pan and roast in oven for 35–40 minutes, basting every 15 minutes, until cooked.

Butterflied Quail with Lemon and Sage

Preheat the oven to 350°F (180°C).

Combine 2 tablespoons of the olive oil, the lemon juice, lemon zest, garlic, pepper and salt in a bowl. Set aside.

Heat the remaining oil in a large pan, add the quail and the chopped sage leaves, and brown quickly. Set aside in a baking dish.

To the pan, add the lemon juice mixture and the chicken stock. Return to the heat, bring to the boil and simmer for 1 minute to reduce, stirring with a wooden spoon.

Pour over the quail and bake for 20–25 minutes. Garnish with whole sage leaves.

3 tablespoons olive oil
1 tablespoon lemon juice
zest of ½ lemon
1 clove garlic, crushed
freshly ground pepper
sea salt
4 quail, butterflied
¼ cup sage, chopped, plus ¼ cup
  whole leaves
¼ cup chicken stock

Casablanca Chicken and Yellow Rice

SERVES 6

3lb 5oz (1½kg) chicken pieces

1oz (30g) butter

2 tablespoons oil

2 large onions, thinly sliced

1 clove garlic, crushed

2in (5cm) piece fresh ginger,
   chopped

¼ teaspoon saffron threads or
   ½ teaspoon turmeric

1 cinnamon stick broken in two

1 cup apricot nectar

½ cup dry white wine

salt and freshly ground black
   pepper

½ cup pitted prunes, soaked

1 cup dried apricots, soaked

1 tablespoon honey

3 teaspoons lemon juice

1 tablespoon toasted sesame
   seeds

Fry chicken pieces in butter and oil until golden, then remove. Fry onions, garlic and spices. Replace chicken, toss in spice onion mixture. Add apricot nectar, wine, salt and pepper.

Cover, cook over moderate heat for 30–40 minutes or until tender. During last 10 minutes add prunes, apricots, honey and lemon juice. Check seasoning. Serve on bed of yellow rice (see recipe). Garnish with extra fruit and sprinkle with sesame seeds.

Candle Nut Chicken

To make the spice paste, first toast the shrimp paste over a gas flame or wrap in foil and toast over a low electric element for 1–2 minutes, turning a few times until browned and slightly crisp.

Place all spice paste ingredients except the candle nuts, leaves and oil in a mortar or food processor and grind to a thick paste. Add the candle nuts and continue to grind until you have a fairly smooth paste.

Heat a wok over medium heat and add the oil. Add the spice paste and leaves and fry for 1–2 minutes until the oil is absorbed.

Now lower the heat to medium-low and continue to fry for 4–5 minutes or until the oil starts to separate again. Stir frequently to prevent burning. Discard the leaves. At this stage, either store the spice paste for later use or continue with the recipe.

Add the chicken to the fried spice paste and stir-fry over medium heat for 4 minutes. Add the salt and sugar and stir.

Add 1 cup of the water and the kaffir lime and turmeric leaves. Bring to the boil, reduce heat to medium-low and cook for 10 minutes, stirring occasionally.

Add the remaining water (or more for a thinner sauce) and cook for a further 5 minutes or until the chicken is cooked. Serve with plain rice.

NOTE
Substitute 6 raw Brazil nuts or 18 blanched raw almonds for candle nuts.

17½oz (500g) chicken pieces (on the bone), cut into about 2in (5cm) pieces

¼ teaspoon salt or to taste

2 teaspoons sugar

1¼ cups water or more

4 kaffir lime leaves

4 turmeric leaves (if available)

CANDLE NUT SPICE PASTE

½ teaspoon shrimp paste

3 teaspoons chilli powder

½ teaspoon ground turmeric

5 scallion (green onion) segments (about 3 tablespoons), chopped

1 tablespoon fresh ginger, roughly chopped

3 cloves garlic, peeled and roughly chopped

1 stalk lemongrass (about 1 tablespoon), chopped

½ teaspoon salt

1 teaspoon palm sugar

10 candle nuts

2 kaffir lime leaves

1 turmeric leaf

2 tablespoons peanut oil

Casserole of Preserved Duck, Pork and Beans

SERVES 6

2lb (1kg) small dried white
  beans, soaked overnight
1 teaspoon dried thyme, leaves
  picked and stalks removed
2 onions, peeled and halved, each
  half stuck with a clove
1 bay leaf
1 bulb garlic, halved crosswise
2 ham hocks
salt and freshly ground black
  pepper
6 legs of confit duck
2 tablespoons fat
1 onion, coarsely chopped
1 tablespoon garlic, minced
2lb (1kg) garlic pork sausage
  links, cut into 2in (5cm) chunks

Drain beans and place in a large stockpot. Add thyme, onion halves, bay leaf, garlic bulb, ham hocks and black pepper. Add cold water to cover by 1¼in (3cm). Bring to a simmer over moderately high heat. Reduce heat to low and cook for 2 hours, adding water as necessary to keep beans barely covered.

Taste beans and add salt if necessary. Remove onion halves and garlic bulb. Strip meat from the ham hocks in large chunks. Transfer beans, bay leaf, and ham to a large earthenware casserole.

Bring duck legs to room temperature, letting excess fat drip off. Wipe duck legs with paper towels.

Preheat oven to 300°F (150°C). In a medium skillet over low heat, melt 2 tablespoons fat. Add chopped onion and minced garlic and sauté for 10 minutes. Add to beans along with sausage and duck legs. Cover loosely with foil and bake for 1¼ hours. Uncover and bake for 30 minutes more. Serve direct from the casserole dish.

Devil Chicken Curry

To make the curry paste, drain the dried chillies and place in a mortar or food processor with all of the remaining spice paste ingredients.

Pound or process until you have a fairly smooth, evenly coloured paste.

Sprinkle the drumsticks with salt and set aside.

Heat the oil in a large pot over medium heat, add the sliced shallots and garlic and fry for about 2 minutes or until the shallots are starting to brown. Add the Curry Paste and mustard seeds and continue to fry, stirring almost constantly for about 5 minutes until aromatic and starting to look a bit oily.

Add the drumsticks, stir well to coat with the curry paste and fry until they start to change colour.

Add the water, bring to the boil then reduce heat to low and simmer for 1 hour or until the chicken is tender.

Stir in the vinegar, dark soy sauce, English mustard and salt to taste.

Serve with plain rice or with coconut rice and a hard-boiled egg as part of a Nasi Lemak meal.

8 large chicken drumsticks

3 tablespoons peanut oil

1 teaspoon salt

6 scallions (green onion) segments (about 3½ tablespoons), sliced

3 cloves garlic, thinly sliced

1 tablespoon black mustard seeds

1½–2 cups water

1½ tablespoons white vinegar

½ tablespoon dark soy sauce

½ tablespoon prepared English mustard

salt to taste

CURRY PASTE

25 large red dried chillies, seeded and soaked in hot water for about 10 minutes to soften

6 fresh red chillies, seeded and roughly chopped

1 cup scallion (spring onion) segments, roughly chopped

3 cloves garlic

2 teaspoons ginger, roughly chopped

8 candle nuts

1 tablespoon ground turmeric

1 tablespoon ground coriander

Chicken and Barley Casserole

SERVES 6

1 cup barley

12 chicken drumsticks

3 whole chillies

1 onion, chopped

2 stalks celery, sliced

30½oz (880g) diced tomatoes in
    juice

salt and freshly ground black
    pepper

6 sprigs parsley

Preheat oven to 350°F (180°C). Place rice in the bottom of a casserole dish. Arrange chicken on top. Wash chillies, trim off stalks and add whole chillies to casserole. Add onion and celery to casserole. Pour tomatoes and juice over casserole. Season with salt and pepper and top with parsley.

Cover and cook for 1 hour. Remove chillies and parsley and serve immediately. If desired, garnish with fresh chillies.

Tandoori Chicken

To make the chilli boh, soak the chillies in boiling water for about 30 minutes until softened.

Place the chillies, liquid, garlic and salt in an electric blender. Blend until you have a smooth sauce.

Mix together the tamarind liquid and salt. Add the curry powder, Chilli Boh and oil, mixing after each addition.

Place the chicken pieces in a large bowl and pour the marinade over. Mix well, cover and set aside for at least 15 minutes (or even overnight). Refrigerate if marinating for a long time.

Preheat the oven to 350°F (180°C).

Remove the chicken from the marinade and place on a rack in a baking dish.

Roast for 30 minutes then increase the heat to 430°F (220°C) and roast for a further 20 minutes or until the chicken is nicely coloured and the juices run clear. Alternatively, cook in a tandoori oven if you are lucky enough to have one! The chicken can also be barbecued.

1 cup Chilli Boh (see below)

½ cup tamarind liquid (soak 1 tablespoon tamarind pulp in ½ cup warm water, stir well and drain off the liquid when cool)

1 teaspoon salt

1 tablespoon Indian meat curry powder

¼ cup vegetable or canola oil

2lb 4oz (1kg) skinless chicken pieces

CHILLI BOH

8 large mild dried red chillies, stems, seeds and membranes removed and roughly chopped

1 cup boiling water

1 large clove garlic

¼ teaspoon salt

Stocks & Consommés

Stock

The basis of a quality soup is a quality stock – it's as simple as that! In years past, a good soup always began with hours of simmering simple vegetables and, perhaps, some meat bones to create a rich broth.

These days, however, if you prefer to bypass this step, there are several prepared stocks available from your local supermarket. They can be found in liquid form, as a paste or as a powder.

Generally speaking, it is much easier to purchase liquid stocks as they have a true flavour and are literally ready to use. Pastes are a good option too because they are concentrated, which allows you to add as much water as necessary to dilute the flavour according to your tastes.

In our opinion, most stock powders should be avoided if the liquid or paste stocks are available. These powders are often heavily salted and therefore offer a salty rather than 'true to taste' flavour. The ratio of powder to water can be difficult to master and some brands contain artificial flavours and colours.

By far the most rewarding and delicious stock is the one you make yourself. Contrary to popular belief, stocks are not difficult to make and, although they do need to simmer for quite some time, their preparation time is minimal.

The following recipes will guide you through the basics of making a good stock – regardless of which type of stock you wish to make, you can follow one of these basic methods. If you have any vegetables in your refrigerator that are looking a little wilted and sad, throw these into the stockpot too as they will add extra flavour and colour.

Oh, and one other thing – remember that stocks freeze extremely well for extended periods of time, so don't be afraid to make a pot of stock when you have large amounts of vegetables, roasted meat bones or turkey frames (from the Christmas bird) on hand. Make the stock and pop it in the freezer for your future risotto or soup.

A stock is a liquid to which bones, meat, vegetables, herbs and spices have imparted their flavour. We always encourage the use of fresh, homemade stocks in all our soup recipes but in this day and age it is unrealistic to expect people to always make their own stock. There are many store-cupboard stocks readily available at the supermarket.

Making good stock is a very simple procedure. The ingredients are simmered in a pot—when strained and degreased the cooking liquid becomes a savoury essence to serve on its own, store for later use, or use in preparing another dish. Recipes for the five basic stocks follow on the next pages. Stock comes from humble beginnings—inexpensive cuts of meat and bones, fish bones and heads, or chicken wings and backs.

Attention to detail will reward you with a rich and tasty stock. All large fat deposits should be removed beforehand, but large bones will give you treasured gelatine, if cracked first, and provide body to your stock.

During cooking, remove scum that occasionally collects on top of the liquid. Scum consist of protein particles released by meat and bones, these float to the surface, where they gather in a foam. As nutritious as it is, the foam must be removed lest it cloud the stock. Skim off the foam as it forms at the start of cooking, skim thereafter only as the recipe directs.

After its initial rapid cooking, stock must not be allowed to return to rapid boil as the turbulence will muddy the liquid. As a final cleansing, the stock should be strained through a fine sieve or a colander lined with muslin.

IMPORTANT TIPS FOR MAKING HOMEMADE STOCK

• Always use cold water.

• Never boil stock. Instead simmer it for a long time so the fat can rise to the top and be skimmed off. If you boil stock it becomes cloudy and greasy as the fat becomes incorporated.

• Adding a little cold water to the stock while it is simmering will help any impurities or scum rise to the surface to be skimmed off.

• It is important to skim off the scum that rises to the surface as you go, topping up with extra water if necessary.

• Brown stock is made from cooked bones and white stock from uncooked or cooked bones.

• Aim for evenly sized chunks of vegetable, meat and bone—they do not have to be perfectly regular, as they eventually will be discarded. However, the smaller the pieces the faster they will flavour the water and the sooner the stock can be used.

• Stock can be reduced for more convenient storage. Reduce the stock by boiling it, uncovered. Stock can be easily reconstituted by the addition of water.

• Stock can be frozen for up to 6 months. Freeze in plastic bags or, if the stock has been reduced, in ice-cube trays.

• Stock can be refrigerated for up to 3 days.

• Never season stock—always save the seasoning for the end result, i.e. the soup you are making.

Chicken Stock (White Stock)

MAKES 52FL OZ (1.5L)

Put all the ingredients in a large stockpot, adding extra water if necessary to ensure the chicken is covered by about 1in (2.5cm) water. Bring to a gentle simmer and continue to simmer for about 1½–2 hours, skimming off any scum with a large spoon, as the stock simmers. Leave to cool slightly before straining through a fine sieve.

NOTE
Giblets can also be added to your stock (for the last half hour of cooking), but always use them sparingly as the flavour can be strong and unpleasant.

1 uncooked chicken carcass or whole chicken about 2lb 4oz (1kg)
3 bay leaves
1 teaspoon black peppercorns
2 celery sticks, leaves included, roughly chopped
2 carrots, unpeeled, chopped
1 onion, unpeeled, halved
3 sprigs thyme
3 pints (2L) cold water

Meat Stock (Brown Stock)

MAKES 52FL OZ (1.5L)

1kg (2lb 4oz) meat bones,
   preferably veal or beef

1 onion, unpeeled, halved

3 bay leaves

1 teaspoon black peppercorns

2 celery sticks, leaves included,
   roughly chopped

1 carrot, unpeeled, chopped

2 tomatoes, chopped

2 sprigs rosemary

3 pints (2L) cold water

Roast the bones in a dry roasting tin at 400°F (200°C) for about 40 minutes. Transfer to a large stockpot and add the remaining ingredients. Place the roasting tin, with a little hot water added, on the hob and heat, stirring until boiling. Boil for 2–3 minutes, scraping any of the sticky residue from the base and sides of the tin. Add this to the stockpot. Cover all the ingredients in the stockpot with water, adding extra if necessary to ensure that everything is covered by about 1in (2.5cm). Bring to a gentle simmer and simmer for about 1½–2 hours. Leave to cool slightly before straining through a fine sieve.

NOTE
Lamb or pork bones should only be used when specifically called for. Their flavour is strong and dominating and may overpower your soup.

Duck Stock

Put all the stock ingredients in a pan and cover with water. Bring to the boil then simmer for 2½ hours, occasionally skimming off any residue. After 2 hours, remove duck and allow to cool. (Leave remaining stock ingredients to simmer for 30 minutes more.)

Strain remaining stock and cool. If possible, chill stock overnight so fat can solidify on top and be easily removed.

1 duck (about 4¾lb/2.2kg)
1 carrot, unpeeled, sliced
2 celery sticks, leaves included,
  roughly chopped
1 bay leaf
3 sprigs parsley
3 sprigs thyme
8 black peppercorns

Veal Stock

*2lb 4oz (1kg) veal shin meat on
the bone, cut into 3in (7.5cm)
pieces*

*4lb 6oz (2kg) veal bones
(preferably knuckles), cracked*

2 carrots

4 stalks celery

3 onions

*4 sprigs fresh thyme, leaves
removed and stalks discarded*

3 unpeeled cloves garlic, crushed

8 black peppercorns

1 bay leaf

Fill a large stock pot halfway with water. Bring the water to the boil, add the veal meat and bones, and blanch them for 2 minutes to clean them.

Drain the meat and bones in a colander, discard the liquid. Rinse the meat and bones under cold running water and return them to the pot.

Wash all the vegetables and slice or chop roughly. Then place in a large stockpot with the veal bones and meat and all remaining ingredients.

Cover with cold water (about 8½ pints/4 litres), bring to the boil and simmer for 2–3 hours, skimming the scum off the surface as it rises to the top.

Add salt to taste, then strain through a sieve lined with absorbent paper or cheesecloth.

Place in a large saucepan and chill until the fat solidifies on the surface. Remove the fat and use or freeze the stock.

Dinner Party Beef Consommé

SERVES 2–3

2oz (60g) butter

1 white onion, finely sliced

14oz (400g) canned beef consommé

1 small carrot, julienned

½ stalk celery, sliced thinly on the diagonal

½ small parsnip, julienned

salt and seasoned pepper blend

2 teaspoons brandy

¼ cup parsley or chives, chopped

In a frying pan, melt the butter and sauté the onion until soft.

Add onion to slow cooker with 1 cup water and all remaining ingredients except brandy and parsley or chives. Simmer for 8 hours on low, ready for serving at dinner.

Add brandy and serve garnished with parsley or chives.

Consommé

Place all ingredients except parsley and sherry in slow cooker and add 12 cups of water. Simmer on low for 8 hours or longer. Allow to stand until cold.

Carefully remove all the fat and take out all large pieces of meat and vegetables, then strain the consommé through gauze or a fine nylon sieve. Serve piping hot with 2 teaspoons of dry sherry in each bowl and a sprinkle of freshly chopped parsley to garnish.

2lb (1kg) lean beef on the bone, such as gravy beef
1 leek, roughly chopped
1 large onion, roughly chopped
2 bay leaves
1 clove garlic, chopped
1 stalk celery with leaves, roughly chopped
3 whole sprigs of parsley, plus ¼ cup, chopped
salt and freshly ground black pepper
¼ cup dry sherry

Index

Published in 2013 by
New Holland Publishers
London • Sydney • Cape Town • Auckland

Garfield House 86–88 Edgware Road London W2 2EA United Kingdom
1/66 Gibbes Street Chatswood NSW 2067 Australia
Wembley Square First Floor Solan Road Gardens Cape Town 8001 South Africa
218 Lake Road Northcote Auckland New Zealand

www.newhollandpublishers.com

A catalogue record of this book is available at the British Library and the National
Library of Australia.

ISBN: 9781742574134

Publisher: Fiona Schultz
Design: Lorena Susak
Production Director: Olga Dementiev
Printer: Toppan Leefung Printing Ltd (China)

10 9 8 7 6 5 4 3 2 1

Images p8-9, p48-49, 72-73, 120-121, p188-189: Shutterstock

Follow New Holland Publishers on
Facebook: www.facebook.com/NewHollandPublishers